LITURGICAL WORSHIP

A LUTHERAN INTRODUCTION

LITURGICAL WORSHIP: A LUTHERAN INTRODUCTION

BY JORDAN COOPER

Copyright 2018 Just and Sinner. All rights reserved. Besides brief quotations, none of this book shall be reproduced without permission.

Permission inquiries may be sent to
JustandSinner@yahoo.com

Just & Sinner
515 East Lincoln Ave.
Watseka, IL 60970

www.JustandSinnerPublishing.com

ISBN-13: 978-0692465776
ISBN-10: 0692465774

TABLE of CONTENTS

Forward	7
The Purpose of Worship	9
Biblical Basis of Liturgical Worship	23
Invocation	35
Confession and Absolution	41
Introit and Kyrie	51
Scripture Readings	57
Gospel Reading and the Sermon	65
Creeds	73
Prayer and the Offering	87
Holy Communion	95
Eucharistic Prayers	103
Words of Institution	111
Distribution of Communion	117
Post-Communion Service	121
Conclusion	125
Bibliography	127
Glossary of Terms	135

FORWARD

I vividly remember the first time I walked into a Lutheran church. Growing up in the Reformed tradition, I had never experienced liturgical worship before. The service was alien to me, with the closest parallel being that Roman Catholic Mass I had attended one time and barely remembered. The music popped up at random points in the service, and the words of the liturgy were chanted. The pastor did not wear the plain black robes that I was used to, but had on something that I thought looked like an ornate poncho. People kept standing and sitting, kneeling and bowing. Some even made the sign of the cross over themselves. I left there with many questions. What did all of this mean? Was this an empty ritual, or did these words and motions mean something?

Only a few weeks later, I found myself back at the same Lutheran church. Eventually, I started attending regularly. Though it took some time to understand the function and benefit of liturgical worship, when I started studying, I quickly found that I could never go back to anything else. Every word was gleaned from the Scriptures. Every movement meant something.

As a new convert to the Lutheran tradition, I was filled with excitement (just as any convert is). The theology, the worship, the history—it was all life-changing. With this newfound vigor, I expected the other congregants to have the same enthusiasm. I was thoroughly disappointed to find that this was simply not the case. What I saw was striking apathy; they had this treasure—these gems of history, of doctrine, of practice—and yet some of them accepted it as merely tradition. Some of them had spent up to eighty years attending a Lutheran church *every week* and still had no understanding about why the elements of worship are the way that they are.

Without an understanding of the meaning of the liturgical elements of a service, these actions become vapid, meaningless motions. There is no benefit in tradition solely for the sake of tradition. This is why there has been such a shift in worship style in recent years. The church in general has moved away from the historic liturgy in favor of something newer, something more appealing to younger generations. If liturgy is nothing more than tradition, then it can change along with the culture just like anything else. What we have seen is that younger generations are not as quick to adopt tradition for the sake of tradition.

This fact changes the landscape of the church and how we bring new people into it.

In the short time that I have been in the ministry, one of the things I have realized is that when people understand the purpose of liturgical worship, they learn to love it. Many understand the basics of the service and its general purpose, but they have not had the opportunity to learn about the history and theology behind each element. This book is born out of a series of studies that I led with my congregation. Though I had not originally intended this to be a book, the extensive outlines that I compiled for my church naturally led to that. Several people urged me to expand and publish these outlines for the purpose of helping other congregations come to a greater knowledge and understanding of the Divine Service.

This book begins with an explanation of Lutheran worship in contrast to other Christian traditions. Then it explores the biblical foundations for worship, proving that Scripture promotes a liturgical form of worship. Following this, it describes each element of the worship service and explains its history and meaning. At the end of the book, I have also included a glossary of terms for those who might be unfamiliar with those terms that are used throughout the book.

This book is meant as a basic introduction and guide to the liturgy. It is not an extensive treatment or scholarly dissertation on liturgical worship (a task I would not be fit for). However, if you find that your appetite has been whetted for more information, I have included an extensive bibliography for additional resources on the topics discussed here. I hope that this book benefits your understanding of worship, and ultimately that of the Triune God who deserves your worship.

As a final note, I want to thank my wife Lisa Cooper for her extensive editing and help throughout the writing of this book.

CHAPTER 1:
The PURPOSE of WORSHIP

Why do Christians go to church? I'm sure we all have other things we could be doing on a Sunday morning instead of shuffling off to a building, surrounded by other Christians, to say some words and sing some songs—right? What is missing here is an understanding of the importance of worship. We are not always conscious about exactly *why* we worship and exactly *what* is supposed to happen when God's people gather together. These questions, however, are central to the Christian life. We are not called to live our Christian life in isolation or devoid of the gathering of believers. We are called to come together in community to worship the God who created us, who redeemed us, who has reconciled us to himself and to each other. The question of the *purpose* of worship, in particular, differentiates various Christian traditions from one another. Before examining specific aspects of Christian liturgy in the Lutheran tradition, we have to first evaluate the current state of worship in the broader contemporary church.

There is a fundamental connection between what a church believes and how a church worships. We sometimes want to disconnect theology and worship in a kind of body/mind dualism, as if we can believe one thing in our minds and act another way with our bodies. There is a common platitude that goes something like, "Evangelical style, Lutheran substance." There is no substance apart from style. Worship simply does not work this way. The mode of worship is not some neutral point concerning which anyone can adapt whatever one wants, suiting one's own desires or interests. As the fifth-century saint Prosper of Aquitaine stated, "The rule of worship is the rule of faith" (*lex orandi, lex credendi*).[1] In other words, worship and belief are intimately connected: how we worship impacts what we believe, and what we believe impacts how we worship.

---

[1] Prosper, *Patrologia Latina*, 51:209–10.

Emotion-Driven Worship

While it is likely that no one would self-consciously claim that his or her worship is driven by his or her emotions, many worship services demonstrate exactly that. In this approach to worship, the Christian is in need of an experience. The gathering in worship then serves to provide an ecstatic experience for all who show up that morning to worship God. The emphasis in this view is the individual's relationship to God rather than one's participation in the corporate interaction between God and the church. The gathering aids the individual's experience, and the church becomes a means to that experiential end.

The churches that promote this experiential view of worship generally have a lengthy time of worship music at the beginning of the service. The songs are chosen not for their theological content but for the mood and tone which they produce. The music then drives one's emotions, causing the worshipper to feel that he or she is experiencing the presence of God. Verses are vapid, and choruses are repeated *ad nauseam*, creating a trance-like state. The Holy Spirit's presence in the service is defined by the feelings of the people in the congregation. If his presence isn't *felt*, then he must not have shown up. Perhaps our worship wasn't *good enough*. Following the long time of worship music, the services generally include a lengthy sermon as well as a time of prayer.

In this approach, the emphasis of worship is upon the heart rather than mind. Theology is downplayed as unimportant or secondary.[2] It does not matter so much what you *believe* but what you *experience*. Your experience then becomes a measuring rod of your spiritual state. If one has an intense display of emotion during the service, including crying, the raising of hands, falling to one's knees, and so forth, that is considered a sign of Christian maturity. If these things do not happen, then perhaps there is a lack of true spirituality.

This view of worship emphasizes the necessity of conversion and of re-conversion. Through the use of music, along with powerful preaching and prayer, unbelievers will be given an opportunity to give their lives to Christ, and those who are in the faith may have an

---

[2] Look, for example, at these lyrics of the popular Christian song "More Like Falling in Love" by Jason Gray: "More than name, faith, or creed / Falling in love with Jesus brought the change in me / ... More like falling in love / Than something to believe in." This type of mentality pits emotion and adherence to creeds against one another, whereas when correctly utilized, emotion and doctrine are not at odds.

opportunity to rededicate their lives to their Lord. The end goal of each service, then, is that people will be convinced to live unto God.[3]

This emotionally-driven approach to worship greatly affects the nature and order of the service. Repetition of prayers, creeds, and chants is not considered a valid way of experiencing God. Instead, worship should be personal and spontaneous. Prayers which are read or recited rather than spoken directly from the heart are generally eschewed as not truly worshipful. Traditional musical instruments, such as organs, are not used because they do not stir the emotions in the same manner as modern instrumentation.

Morally Driven Worship

In the view of some Christians, the church primarily functions as an ethical community. The confessions of particular doctrines, then, are rendered unimportant. A common phrase of these churches is "Deeds, not creeds."[4] The message of Jesus is reduced to moralistic instruction on how to live, usually with an emphasis on love. This form of worship excludes the content of what Christians believe and focuses solely on societal change. Jesus is therefore a new Moses: a new and better law-giver. He created the church only as a way to serve and change the world, absent of any theological or doctrinal content.[5]

Christianity has always had an important ethical dimension, as God calls his people to a certain standard of life which is set apart from the broader world in which Christians live.[6] In a biblical approach, however, the ethical aspect of Christian existence is secondary to the saving and redeeming work of Christ. Throughout the centuries, there

---

[3] This type of worship has roots, particularly, in the Second Great Awakening, which swept through the United States in the early nineteenth century. Preachers like Charles Finney emphasized the necessity of personal conversion and emotional experience through moving music, as well as the use of the "anxious bench" for those who were moved by the service. See Finney, *Autobiography*.

[4] It is unclear where this statement first came from, but it has been used by the popular writer Rick Warren to describe what he sees as a "new reformation." See Horton, "Creeds and Deeds."

[5] It is true that, in a sense, Jesus is a new and greater Moses. Along with giving the law, Moses was also an instrument of salvation and redemption for the people of Israel. Moses' *primary* role, however, was his giving of the law, whereas Christ's primary role is in bringing salvation from the law's condemnation.

[6] See Harless, *A System of Christian Ethics*, for a Lutheran approach to the subject.

have been many churches and theologians who have downplayed the saving work of Jesus, focusing exclusively on ethical formation in the individual believer's life.

One time in which this happened on a large scale was during the rise of Protestant liberalism in the nineteenth century. The famous German philosopher Immanuel Kant argued that religion was useful for the purpose of keeping morality in check. A number of theologians, such as Albrecht Ritschl (one of the most important theologians of the nineteenth century), argued that Kant was essentially correct, and that the Christian faith is centered on moral living.[7] For many liberal theologians, this meant that the supernatural events explained in Scripture, such as the miracles of Jesus, and even the resurrection, are not essential to the Christian faith.[8] They merely serve to help the proclamation of ethical living.[9]

The moralistic approach to the Christian faith has a profound impact on the worship life of the church. Rather than emphasizing the saving work of Christ, the church seeks to better the lives of its members and to change the world in a positive manner. Preaching, then, will emphasize Christian living or social issues rather than the redemptive work of Christ. The issues emphasized will depend upon the particular culture in which one is living. In the nineteenth century, this strain of theology tended to emphasize particular enlightenment ideals and even led several German theologians to support World War I.[10] In the twentieth century, this type of preaching began to connect itself with liberation theology, which emphasized the need for social justice toward oppressed people groups.[11] In contemporary society, liberal churches

---

[7] Kant's major work in this area was his book *Religion within the Bounds of Reason Alone*.

[8] The most helpful work available in terms of comparing Ritschl's theology to that of Lutheranism is Lotz, *Ritschl and Luther*.

[9] During the nineteenth century, a number of theologians began writing what they argued were accurate biographies of Jesus. These biographies were created by deciphering the true from false material in the gospels, usually by eliminating all supernatural elements. Schweitzer's *The Quest of the Historical Jesus* is the classic work on this subject.

[10] Karl Barth overviews all of these ideas in *Protestant Theology in the Nineteenth Century*. His criticisms led Barth to formulate what is often labeled "neo-orthodoxy" in response to Protestant liberalism.

[11] Liberation theology stems from the work of Roman Catholic theologian Gustavo Gutierrez, and in particular, his book *Liberation Theology*. Though the movement originated in Latin America, it has become popular in Western Europe

now often emphasize feminism and homosexual rights.[12]

Morally focused worship does not only affect liberal churches, however; it is also sometimes identified with traditional Christian morality. One might emphasize biblical sexual ethics, for example, from the pulpit to such an extent that the preaching of Christ is no longer central.[13] This ethical focus means that the service is not centered on what God does for sinners, but instead, it is centered on what people do for God or for the world around them.

Seeker-Driven Worship
The twentieth century saw the rise of a new, unique approach to worship, in which the service is aimed not primarily at believers but at those who do not believe. This approach was popularized in the 1970s through the 1990s as a model of church growth. It is often described as "seeker-sensitive."[14] In this approach, the purpose of worship is not for those who are already part of the Christian church, but for those who are outside of the faith. Discipleship is deemphasized from the pulpit, and sermons are preached with the unbelieving person in view.

At first glance, this approach to worship might seem like a positive move in the church. Jesus certainly promoted the importance and necessity of evangelism toward those who are lost in sin (Matt. 28:18–20). However, though evangelism is a central element of the church, it is not the primary purpose of the worship service itself. Some missiologists (those who study missions) have distinguished between two different models of evangelism.[15] One is an "attractional" model, wherein the church seeks to make itself attractive to unbelievers. Here, the goal of the church is to make worship an attractive place for unbelievers, and

---

and the Unites States through theologians such as Jurgen Moltmann (see *Theology of Hope*).

[12] These movements, called "feminist theology" and "queer theology," are an outgrowth of liberation theology. For an example of a work that combines the approach of these movements, see Lightsey, *Our Lives Matter*.

[13] This is one of the problems with the growth of the religious right under the influence of Jerry Falwell. While ethical and political issues are important, they should never become the church's *central* proclamation, which should always remain the cross of Christ.

[14] See Dobson, *Seeker-Sensitive Service*.

[15] See Whitesel, *Organix*, 121–38. This excerpt is also available at https://churchhealthwiki.wordpress.com/2014/11/11/incarnational-vs-attractional-what-is-the-difference-organixbook/.

when an unbeliever attends, he or she will receive salvation. The other model is described as "incarnational." In this approach, Christians are to live as Christ in the midst of the culture around them and bring the gospel to those outside the church through their ordinary lives and vocations. How a church views the nature and purpose of evangelism will impact how a worship service is conducted.

One of the convictions underlying the seeker-driven approach to worship is that genuine God-seekers exist. This conviction itself seems to contradict Scripture, which clearly states that no one seeks God (Rom. 3:11). Instead, it is God who seeks and saves sinners. Because of its mistaken perspective, the seeker-driven movement tries to make worship an entertaining event so that unbelievers will desire to attend services, and consequently, make a decision to become Christians. These seeker-driven churches eschew traditional forms of worship in favor of those which are entertaining. Big productions, loud music, videos, and sermons about movies are common. These tactics flow from the desire to bring people to church and consequently bring them to Christ.

In seeker-driven churches, heavy scriptural exposition and theological content are viewed as suspect in a Sunday morning service, because the church is not called to equip and disciple God's saints through preaching and teaching. Instead, people are called to disciple themselves.[16] The pastors must then preach basic messages that will attract and be understandable to the unbeliever.

Roman Catholic Worship

The previous three approaches to worship are common within contemporary Protestant churches. The Roman Catholic tradition, however, has a much different view of the purpose of worship than churches arising from the Protestant Reformation. Though similar to Lutheran and Anglican worship in form, the purpose and emphasis of Roman Catholic worship differs from that of other liturgical traditions.

At the heart of the Roman Catholic tradition is the sacrifice of the Mass. In this view, the central act of worship is the Holy Eucharist. The primary purpose of the Eucharist, however, is not simply to be received by congregants, but to be sacrificed upon the altar. In this perspective, the bread and wine are transubstantiated (changed) into the true body and blood of Christ. The body and blood of Christ are then offered by the

---

[16] DeVries, "Self Feeder."

priest to God the Father on the altar as an unbloody sacrifice for sins.[17] The death of Christ on Calvary is re-presented at every Mass. The direction of worship, then, is from the priest to God. The Eucharist is a sacrifice which one offers to God, not only a gift of God to the sinner.

Many of these differences between Lutheran and Roman Catholic worship arise from the unique view of the priesthood which is apparent in Roman Catholic theology. In this tradition, the priest receives the sacrament of ordination, and an indelible character is placed on him. Something about the person himself is changed, and he becomes an *alter Christus* (another Christ). The priest then functions in a special manner before God on behalf of the church. The sacramental authority of the church is granted to the successors of the apostles (the bishops) and granted to the priests. Roman Catholicism does not affirm the priesthood of all believers in the sense that various Protestant traditions do.

Due to the nature and importance of the priesthood in Roman Catholic theology, the worship service is centered on the act of the priest himself, with less emphasis on congregational participation. This is why for a long time in the Roman Church, the laity did not receive wine during Holy Communion. They received only Christ's body, while the priest partook of both elements on behalf of the people. Since the central act of the service is the priest's offering the sacrifice to God rather than the actual partaking of Christ's body and blood by the people, private Masses, where no one is present other than the priest himself, are held in order to benefit particular people for whom the priest is offering Christ's body and blood.

While the Roman Catholic service might look similar to a Lutheran or Anglican one, there is a vast difference between the Roman Catholic and Protestant traditions. In the Roman view, there is a higher emphasis on what the priest offers to God rather than what God offers to his people in Word and Sacrament. Protestant liturgical churches emphasize congregational participation in worship, whereas the Roman church does not do so to the same extent.

Reformed Worship

---

[17] "As a sacrifice of expiation the Mass effects both the remission of sins and the punishment due to sins" (Baker, *Fundamentals of Catholicism* III:269). Pages 229–74 in the volume referenced here contain a helpful explanation of the Roman teaching on Holy Communion.

During the time of the Reformation, there was a large divide between two Protestant traditions: Lutheran and Reformed. Martin Luther retained the basic structure of the Roman Catholic Mass, while eliminating elements which were at odds with the gospel and contradictory to Scripture.[18] The Reformed, on the other hand, rejected the medieval worship service altogether and sought to create a new form of worship based strictly on the New Testament commandments.[19]

This approach to worship, which is found in Presbyterian, Dutch Reformed, and other Calvinist churches, emphasizes the glory of God in worship. Congregants gather together to glorify God by their actions and do so only in ways that God has strictly commanded. This approach, known as the *regulative principle of worship*, states that Christians are to do in worship only those things which God has commanded in the New Testament. Any deviation from those practices, they argue, denies God the glory that he is due from his people in a worship service.

The result of this perspective on worship is that the service is very plain. Many Reformed churches do not have art in a worship setting, since the utilization of art is not commanded. They reject, especially, images of Jesus as a violation of the Second Commandment (the second half of the First Commandment for Lutherans). It has been said that worship for the Puritans was "four bare walls and a sermon."[20] While it might be a slight exaggeration, this phrase demonstrates a genuine difference between Calvinism and other traditions.

Much of the Reformed tradition is strictly Sabbatarian, meaning that it argues for a strict Sabbath observance on Sunday, often called the Lord's Day.[21] This day is reserved for worship alone, and neither work nor amusements should be done. Many congregations have both a Sunday morning and a Sunday evening service in order to emphasize the

---

[18] See Zeedon and Walker, *Faith and Act*, on the continuity of the Lutheran Reformation with earlier medieval traditions.
[19] See Ritchie, *Regulative Principle*, for an introduction to this issue. An opposing reformed view, which modifies the regulative principle, can be found from John Frame, and R. J. Gore in *Covenantal Worship*.
[20] I have been unable to find the origin of this phrase, though it is commonly cited.
[21] This notion remains heavily debated, especially within the Presbyterian Church of America. While the Westminster Confession follows a strict Sabbatarian principle, many pastors take exception to this. The Orthodox Presbyterian Church, in contrast to the PCA, holds to a strict subscription to the confessional documents, and thus is Sabbatarian. A defense of the traditional view can be found in Pipa, *The Lord's Day*.

importance of Sabbath observance.

Churches that are in this tradition have a simplified liturgical form. The service begins with a call to worship, followed by a confession of sins that changes weekly. There is no absolution, but a declaration of pardon, which is usually a passage from Scripture that speaks about God's mercy and forgiveness. In some churches, only psalms are sung during worship, and instruments are not used since they are not commanded in the worship of the church.[22] In other congregations, hymns are sung which are heavily theological in content. The preaching is generally lengthy and includes an in-depth explanation of a particular biblical text. Sermons tend to be more academic than those in other traditions, following the structure of a lecture or Bible study.

There are a variety of nuances to worship in the Reformed tradition, since this approach to worship has been developed over a period of 500 years. Worship is simple, and the primary emphasis is the glory of God. God is the sovereign and holy Lord, and in worship, one acknowledges God's majesty by worshipping him strictly in the manner that he has prescribed.

Other Approaches to Worship
In a short survey such as this, it is impossible to explain all the various nuances and perspectives on an important issue like worship. In many congregations, a variety of the above views are present. Many seeker-sensitive churches, for example, are also emotionally driven in their worship method and moralistic in their preaching. There are also churches in the Reformed tradition that do not adhere strictly to the regulative principle and use elements of other forms of worship.[23]

There are also several other Christian traditions that have their own unique perspectives on Christian worship that have not been explained here. The Anabaptists, for example (now known primarily through the Mennonites and Amish), promote a stricter form of the

---

[22] Exclusive psalmody is not as popular as it once was but remains the practice of the Reformed Presbyterian Church of North America and of some Scottish Presbyterian churches. Two modern defenses of this practice can be found in Schwertley, *Exclusive Psalmody* and Bushell, *Songs of Zion*.

[23] John Frame, as cited previously, is an example of this more moderate approach. There are also some in the Federal Vision movement who argue for a more liturgical and traditional approach to worship than has been practiced in Reformed churches historically. See Meyers, *The Lord's Service*.

regulative principle of worship, holding to a more simplified form of worship than any other tradition.[24] Some, such as the Exclusive Brethren, have house churches, with no particular structure of worship; they also do not have pastors.[25]

The worship of the Eastern Orthodox churches has not been described here, though some elements of their liturgy are explored later in the book. The Eastern Orthodox emphasize worship as the joining together of heaven and earth and as participation in the life of God, which culminates in the Eucharist.[26] Several of these themes are echoed in Lutheran thought. Another branch of the Reformation, Anglicanism, has a variety of traditions of worship, many of which are similar to those of the Lutheran perspective. There is a difficulty in explaining Anglican worship, however, because perspectives vary between movements within Anglicanism. While traditional Anglican theologians draw from both Lutheran and Reformed ideas, Anglo-Catholicism is similar to Roman Catholicism in its view of worship.[27]

Lutheran Worship

Like all other Christian traditions, Lutheranism has its own perspective on the purpose and nature of Christian worship. An understanding of this perspective demonstrates why Lutheran worship looks and feels so different from worship services in other churches. At the center of Lutheran worship is a dialogue between God and man. The human creature confesses his unworthiness to enter before a holy God. Consequently, God shows his great mercy in giving forgiveness to the repentant sinner, and the believer then responds with words of thanksgiving and praise. This back-and-forth dialogue of God's giving forgiveness and the congregation's offering thanks continues throughout the entire service.

Most Christians are uncomfortable with the idea that people should, in any sense, go to church in order to receive something from God. This idea might seem rather selfish. Does this not make worship about us rather than God? Instead, shouldn't we be offering all that we

---

[24] See Roth, *Practices*.
[25] Unfortunately, the title "Exclusive Brethren" is often identified with a cult-like sectarian group called the Plymouth Brethren Christian Church. This is not the group I refer to.
[26] See Hopko, *Worship*.
[27] See Dunlop, *Public Worship*.

have to God? While this objection might sound pious, it is misguided. Between God and man, who is really in need? Does God *need* anything from us? Is he not sufficient in and of himself? Is there anything possibly worthwhile that we can give God which will truly benefit him? In reality, it is not God who is in need, but *we* are in need. We are in need of grace, mercy, and forgiveness, and these things are what God desires to give! While it is true that in the worship service, the congregation offers praise to God, at the center of worship is the grace which God gives to sinners.

In many churches, the service begins with an extensive time of worship music praising God as God. But what is one worshipping God *for*? In Scripture, the worship of God is never abstract but is in response to specific actions of deliverance. For example, God does not give the Ten Commandments to the people of Israel until he redeems them from their Egyptian captors. The obedience offered by the Jews is in response to God's deliverance. In the same way, worship during a liturgical service is done in response to God's previous works of deliverance. God proclaims absolution through the mouth of the pastor, and the congregation offers God praise in response. We then confess our need of God's mercy in the *Kyrie* and respond in praise again with the *Gloria*. We receive God's grace in Holy Communion and then again offer praise and thanksgiving in light of his gifts.

Differences between Lutheran Worship and that of Other Traditions

Worship in the Lutheran tradition is viewed differently than in the other traditions as described above. First, emotion does not drive the worship of the Lutheran church. Emotion is not a bad thing; the good news of Jesus Christ is certainly something to get emotional about! The problem is not in emotion itself, or in being moved by the love of God as expressed throughout the service; the problem is when emotion is the *driving force* of worship. One's spiritual state is not determined by emotion, and feelings should not guide the service. In a fallen world, emotions often waver, and something more steady and permanent must ground the church.

The center of Lutheran worship is God's gifts to sinners. Therefore, the morally driven worship model is rejected. Ethics, like emotion, is a good and important part of God's creation. The Bible does contain ethical commands, and it is the duty of the pastor to preach on them. Moral commandments are not, however, the *center* of worship.

Ethics and Christian morality are always to be taught in view of the gospel, which is always the central aspect of Christian worship. Ethical living is a response to the grace that God shows sinners in Christ.

Seeker-driven worship is directly opposed to Lutheran theology and practice. The first and most obvious reason this is the case is that in a Lutheran view, there are no seekers. Man does not search for God, but God searches for man. Faith is not a product of the human will, but it is God's free gift of grace. Thus, the premise of seeker-driven worship is unbiblical. Seeker-driven churches also tend to place elements in worship for the purpose of entertainment. In the front of the church is a stage and a variety of performers, including the pastor and musicians. The congregation is then more like an audience than an actual congregation. The back-and-forth dialogue between God and man is completely absent in this view.

The differences between Roman Catholic and Lutheran worship have been explained in many different books and documents since the sixteenth century.[28] The two traditions share a common liturgical heritage, and a Roman Catholic Mass looks similar to a Lutheran Divine Service. However, there are some important theological differences. While Lutherans have sometimes referred to their worship service as a Mass, Lutheranism has always rejected the concept of the *sacrifice* of the Mass.[29] Christ's work of salvation happened once for all. It does not need to be repeated, or re-presented, on the altar of the church. Moreover, the Lord's Supper is God's gift to us, not our offering to God. The Roman Church changes the proper direction of worship.

Finally, the Lutheran view of worship differs from that of the Reformed tradition.[30] The Reformed emphasize the glory of God in worship, whereas Lutherans focus on God's grace given in Word and Sacrament. This is not to say that Lutherans are not concerned with God's glory, or that Reformed Christians do not talk about God's grace. The emphasis of each church, however, does differ, and this fact is apparent in the manner in which worship functions. Lutherans do not hold to a strict view of how one must worship, but they allow for some variation in practice, the use of images, and other things which are not

---

[28] Perhaps the most detailed remains the classic work *Examination of the Council of Trent*, by Martin Chemnitz.
[29] However, there certainly is a sacrifice of praise as part of the worship service.
[30] I addressed these differences in Cooper, *The Great Divide*, 89–108.

condemned in Scripture. This is not to say that Lutheran worship is simply a free-for-all, or that biblical commands regarding worship are irrelevant to the worship life of the church. Instead, Scripture itself presents a theology of worship which is best practiced in a liturgical service.

Conclusion

As we examine the various aspects of worship in a Lutheran setting, these important differences between Christian views of worship will continue to demonstrate why the structure of a Lutheran Divine Service differs from that of other churches. In worship, God comes down to us and gives us his grace, and we respond in thanksgiving and praise.

Liturgical Worship

CHAPTER 2:
The BIBLICAL BASIS of LITURGICAL WORSHIP

It is a common assumption that liturgical worship is merely a church tradition. I have heard many people say that early Christians exercised spontaneity during their worship services, and at some point during the Middle Ages, Christians became rigid and ritualistic in their worship practices, thus departing from the life of the early church. There are congregations that claim to be worshipping as did the church in Acts (in other words, the *right* way to worship) who argue that all of the structured elements of worship were later additions. They believe that those Christians who still worship in a liturgical manner are indebted more to the medieval Roman Catholic Church than they are to Holy Scripture.[31] This whole idea is mistaken. While the liturgical service, in the manner it is practiced today, did take centuries to reach its current form, liturgical worship itself is found in the pages of Scripture. The current form of a liturgical service is founded on a number of fundamental principles found in the Old and New Testaments.

Worship in the Old Testament
Worship is a central biblical theme and thus extends throughout both testaments. Like any other biblical theme, the foundation is laid beginning with the Old Testament and finds its fulfillment in the New Testament. The Old Covenant reveals a basic structure of worship upon which the New Testament authors build.

God gave the nation of Israel a very particular mode and model of

---

[31] This view is especially popular within various restorationist movements. There were several groups in the nineteenth century that claimed that there was some kind of great apostasy in the early church—sometimes identified with the conversion of Emperor Constantine in the fourth century—and that all developed traditions should be rejected in order to return to the pure, uncorrupted worship of the apostles. This idea is popular today in the Churches of Christ.

worship. Israel was unique among the nations in its time since God chose that specific people group in which he would work redemption for the world. There were worshippers of Yahweh outside the national boundaries of Israel who did not have the same theocratic structure. Thus, their worship likely looked different from that in Israel. The worship of Israel in particular, however, is prototypical of the worship of God's people in the church, specifically as centered on the atoning death of Christ.

One aspect of worship in Israel was that the people functioned on sacred time.[32] There was a holy day each week—the Sabbath—in which all people in Israel would gather to worship Yahweh as they ceased their ordinary daily work. The entire week revolved around this singular day of worship. Not only did the week revolve around worship, but so did the yearly calendar. God appointed a number of specific feasts for the people of Israel to celebrate. Through these feasts, the Jews remembered and commemorated the redemptive acts of God as they looked forward to the coming Messiah. There are seven appointed feasts described in the Old Testament: Passover, Unleavened Bread, Firstfruits, the Feast of Weeks, the Feast of Trumpets, and the Feast of Booths. Each of these holy times had its own unique purpose and emphasis for the people of Israel.

At the center of these feasts was the Passover, wherein the people remembered the time when the angel of death passed over those whose doorposts were covered in the blood of the lamb. It is important to note that the Jews did not view this event simply as an intellectual remembrance, but they believed that in some mysterious way, they became part of the people who were redeemed during the Exodus. They were partaking in that redemptive event, even though time separated them from the Jews during the Mosaic era. This event was a prefiguration of the death of Christ, the true and final Lamb of God whose life was given so that those who are covered by his blood might escape death.[33] Holy Communion is, then, the church's weekly Passover, wherein the people of God participate in the redemption won on Calvary.

God also prescribed a number of specific ways in which the

---

[32] Some helpful resources for understanding Old Testament worship as prescribed in the Pentateuch are Kleinig, *Leviticus*, Morales, *Who Shall Ascend*, and Sklar, *Leviticus*.

[33] This connection between Passover and Christ is an ancient one. The church father Melito of Sardis (died around 180) wrote about this connection in his work *Peri Pascha* (*ANF* 8:750–62).

people of Israel were to worship and honor him. At the heart of worship is sacrifice. The idea of sacrifice predates the nation of Israel, as Genesis describes the importance of sacrifice at the time of Cain and Abel (Gen. 4:3–5).[34] Other saints, such as Noah and Abraham, also offered sacrifices to God as an act of worship. This theme of sacrifice is expounded in the Mosaic covenant, as God prescribed very specific sacrifices for a number of sins. The book of Leviticus describes this large variety of sacrifices, including guilt offerings, burnt offerings, and peace offerings. These sacrifices were offered on account of the sins of the people, and due to their temporary and imperfect nature, the sacrifices were offered repeatedly. Though the language of the Old Testament, at times, might make it seem as if these sacrifices are efficacious to remove sins, they do so only in a typological manner. In other words, the sacrifices did not forgive sins in and of themselves, but only as they pointed forward to the once-for-all sacrifice of Christ on Calvary. It is only Christ's perfect sacrifice which removes sin.

Along with sacrifices for sin, the Jews also offered thank-offerings to God. These offerings were not performed in order to mend one's relationship to God, but they presuppose that such a relationship has already been established. While the burnt and guilt offerings were prescribed for specific times, with respect to both one's personal sins and the broader Jewish calendar, the thank-offerings were not.[35] These sacrifices are free actions of the worshipper, whereby the faithful Jew offers up a sacrifice as a way to thank God for blessings that God has bestowed upon the believer. This idea of thank-offering is essential in New Testament worship and is at the heart of the liturgical service of the church.

One of the most important aspects of the Jewish life of worship was the order of the priesthood which God established through the line of Levi. God set aside a particular group of men to be used as his priests and prescribed exactly what these priests were called to do and to wear. In Exodus 28, God commands a specific uniform to be worn by those who are placed into the holy office of the priesthood, including "a breastplate, an ephod, a robe, a skillfully woven tunic, a turban, and a sash" (Ex. 28:1–4). There are then a number of more specific instructions throughout this

---

[34] For more on this topic, see Chytraeus, *On Sacrifice*.
[35] These thank-offerings are usually labeled either the "peace-offering" or the "fellowship offering."

chapter regarding how these garments are to be made and worn. When God established the Levitical priesthood, he was concerned not simply about the matters of the heart, but also how the priests dressed and conducted worship. Everything was to be done in a particular and reverent manner.

One aspect of Levitical worship was music. Music has always been an important part of worship. The Israelites played music while offering up sacrifices to God, along with incense, as an aspect of the divinely commanded ritual. God made music so important in worship, in fact, that he inspired a hymnal to be used by the people of God. While the writing and singing of songs to God is a practice which predates the Psalms (see the Song of Moses in Ex. 15, for example), the primary means by which Israel worshipped God was through the Psalter. These songs were sung so often that the worshippers in Israel likely had them all memorized. Music remains an essential part of Christian worship, as do the Psalms in particular.

Although these standards of Old Testament worship were commanded, Christians today are not called to copy every aspect of Levitical ritual. These elements of worship in the Old Testament were largely typological, meaning that they pointed forward to something greater: the life, death, and resurrection of Christ. Modern Christians, for example, are not called to offer animal sacrifices on behalf of sin. Christ's work on the cross was the final sacrifice, and it does not need to be repeated. This does not mean, however, that Old Testament worship is in a *completely* different form than is worship today. Worship in the Old Covenant was organized, formal, and reverent. Though many aspects of worship have changed due to the coming of Christ, there are no grounds for arguing that these fundamental principles have changed. As the worship of the New Testament and the early church are examined, it is clear that ways of worship in the Old and New Testaments have an intimate connection to one another.

Heavenly Worship

When speaking about worship in the early church, Christians often turn to the book of Acts seeking an exact model of worship which the contemporary church is to follow. While Acts certainly gives the church important information about the early formation of the Christian faith, and thus of worship, it is not meant to be a worship manual. Many Christians tend to argue today that the house-churches in Acts, for example, are a divinely ordained law which all believers should implement.³⁶ This is not necessarily the case. Early Christians did not meet in homes because this is the ideal location and mode of worship. They worshipped there out of *necessity*. We live in a situation where the church has freedom to have its own buildings, structure its own form and order of worship, and make vestments. One should not assume that the lack of such freedom is necessarily purer.

Rather than using the book of Acts as a worship guide and manual for the church, Christians should look to the most extensive treatment of worship in the New Testament: the book of Revelation. This may seem like an odd starting point for such a discussion. Revelation is just a collection of end-times prophecies, right? Though it does indeed have a prophetic element, scattered throughout the book of Revelation are descriptions of worship in heaven. While modern Christians often look at the Apocalypse as a frightening book predicting immanent destruction upon the world, the apostle John wrote the book in a very different context from our own. He wrote to a church in the midst of persecution, assuring the people that no matter how much they suffered—no matter how bad the persecution would get—Jesus Christ has the victory. It is a book not of despair, but of heavenly hope.³⁷

Worship in heaven is a continual reality. This heavenly worship is one of the ways that John illustrates the hope of heaven. While life in this age may look disastrous from an earthly perspective, there is a plan at work which the human eyes cannot see. Christ is continually reigning on his throne, and the angelic creatures and saints in heaven are worshipping the Lamb every day. In the midst of destruction and death in this world, the reality of heaven is among us. When the saints worship together in a church service, there is a union between heaven and earth. Believers are not worshipping alone but are together alongside others in the throne room of Christ. We sing, we rejoice, we pray, and we worship with the angels, archangels, and martyrs. There is an intimate connection between heavenly worship and the worship of the saints on earth. In the Divine Service, the church militant and the church triumphant are united. Heavenly worship, then, is the pattern for the church's worship

---

³⁶ See Atkerson, *House Church*.
³⁷ On Revelation, see Brighton, *Revelation*; Franzmann, *Revelation*; and Hahn, *The Lamb's Supper*. Though Hahn is Roman Catholic, his connections between the liturgy and heavenly worship are helpful.

life. This is the kind of worship which, unlike Levitical worship, is eternal. This worship will never pass away.

Worship in the book of Revelation is fundamentally liturgical. It has a set form and pattern: certain words are used at particular times, appropriate prayers are offered, specific postures are required of worshippers. It becomes clear when one investigates the different aspects of worship in the book of Revelation that there is a striking difference between this type of worship and the style of worship found in most contemporary Protestant churches. Worship in heaven is more closely likened to the historic liturgy found in the Lutheran church than other, more contemporary versions.

The first worship scene in the book of Revelation is in chapter 4, in which John describes Christ seated on a throne around the crystal sea. Around Jesus, there are a number of worshippers present, including the "living creatures" and the twenty-four elders. These beings are shown reciting particular words in their acts of worship. The living creatures cry out,

> Holy, holy, holy,
> Lord God Almighty,
> Who was and is and is to come! (Rev. 4:8)

For some contemporary worshippers, one's praise is not sincere if it consists of repetition or of pre-written words. These people argue that God does not desire specific patterns of language, but instead, he wants to hear spontaneous words of praise that come out of the overflow of one's heart. The creatures in Revelation 4:8, however, repeat this same phrase day and night, without rest! When a church includes written prayers and words of praise which are repeated or used each service, its practice is consistent with the worship John describes of the living creatures before the Lamb of God.

It is not only the living creatures who worship in this manner. The twenty-four elders are also said to use a specific phrase in worship:

> You are worthy, O Lord,
> To receive glory and honor and power;
> For You created all things,
> And by Your will they exist and were created." (Rev. 4:11)

While this text does not state that the elders recited these same words each day and night, it is apparent, again, that these are memorized words. It is not that one elder says these words spontaneously, but that all of them repeat this phrase together. When a congregation speaks specific words together during a service, it is reflecting the worship of the twenty-four elders. They do not simply worship God on their own, or with their own unique words, but together with the family of God. The way this worship is to be done is through written words and songs of praise.

Along with the recitation of these words of praise, there are other liturgical actions in which the elders are engaged. They all lay down their crowns before the Lamb, and again, they do so together. This is a liturgical action, whereby the elders honor Christ as the great king through their symbolic laying down of crowns before God's throne. These elders are also said to "fall down" (Rev. 4:10) before the throne of Christ, prostrating themselves in honor of his holiness. This act demonstrates two important principles: first, that worship includes symbolic actions whereby the glory of Christ is magnified; and second, that worship includes bodily actions such as prostration. Liturgical churches employ the entire body in worship. People may stand, sit, kneel and even prostrate themselves in the context of the worship service.

Similarly, incense is frequently described in the book of Revelation as an aspect of worship. In the Old Testament, incense was used especially in connection to sacrifices and prayer. Incense engages the sense of smell, which is often neglected in modern Christian services. In Revelation 5, the living creatures and the elders are said to have golden bowls full of incense, which are identified with the prayers of the saints offered to God. Therefore, incense is not only for Old Testament worship, but it is used in heaven alongside of prayer. Some Christians argue that incense should not be used in modern worship because it was connected with the Old Testament sacrificial system. Since Christ was the final sacrifice for sins, incense is no longer needed. This text from Revelation demonstrates, however, that incense endures in heaven, where no sacrifices for sin are offered. Incense is tied not only to animal sacrifice, but also to prayer. As long as prayer endures, so does the use of incense.

In the context of the broader Protestant world, Lutheranism is unique in another way: Lutheran worship uses an altar. During the Reformation, Martin Luther retained much of the ceremony surrounding worship in the Middle Ages, including the use of an altar. On the altar,

Holy Communion is celebrated and prayers are offered. The Reformed tradition, in contrast, rejected the use of an altar and chose instead to use a table for the Lord's Supper. Because in the Roman Catholic Church the Eucharist is viewed as a sacrifice that the priest offers to God, for the Reformed, the presence of an altar in the church is often tied to that idea. In order to distance themselves from the Roman Catholic view, the Reformed removed altars entirely. In the same vein, the Reformed argue that the altar is connected to the Old Testament sacrifices, and since there is no longer any need for animal sacrifice, an altar has been rendered unnecessary.

In the book of Revelation, however, an altar is connected to heavenly worship and *not* to animal sacrifice. The place where incense is offered, being the prayer of the saints, is on the altar (Rev. 8:3–5). Clearly, in heaven, there is no need for sacrifice, but the altar remains. This heavenly altar is the place where the saints' prayers are offered, which is why in Lutheran worship the prayers of the church are made at the altar. This heavenly altar is before the very throne of God. It is the gateway to Christ's presence. Altars in Lutheran congregations are also often surrounded by candles, which are described throughout the Apocalypse as a prominent item in heaven (Rev. 1:12). Ultimately, in the church, the altar is the place where heaven and earth meet, because this is where Christ's body and blood are present and where the prayers of the saints are offered up to God in his heavenly throne room.

Along with the use of incense and an altar, other elements of Old Testament worship are mentioned in the Apocalypse of St. John. As in the Levitical priesthood, certain garments are connected to worship. In the worship scene of Revelation 4, the elders are described as clothed in white robes and wearing golden crowns. White robes are later mentioned in Revelation 6:11 and 7:14. In the first instance, the reference is to the martyrs of God who worship under the altar, and who upon their deaths are granted white robes. In the second reference, it is apparent that these robes are not the unique garments of the twenty-four elders and the martyrs, but that they are granted to all of the saints. The robes are washed "white in the blood of the lamb." These robes serve as a symbol of purity and cleansing. The darkness of sin is taken away, and the saints are presented as pure to God the Father. Today, a white robe, known as an alb, is worn in a liturgical worship service by the pastor, the acolytes, the readers, and those helping to serve communion. In this way, those in front of the church serve as a reminder of the gospel, as their garments express the purity of the saints who are washed in the blood of Christ.

The worship portrayed in the book of Revelation is thoroughly liturgical in nature. The saints and angels use repetitious memorized prayers, sing together, and bow at certain times in worship. An altar is present on which incense and prayers are offered. The saints are arrayed in white robes. All of these elements reflect a liturgical service as normative for the church, for the model of worship is heaven, and in earthly worship, heaven and earth are united. For those who reject liturgical forms of worship, an argument must be made that the form of worship greatly differs in the church from that of Israel and in heaven. Although in Jewish worship and in heavenly worship, God desires to have repetitious prayers, singing, incense, an altar, and so forth, for some reason, these aspects of worship have ceased in this intermediate period on earth following the Israelite kingdom and prior to the consummation of God's kingdom at the coming of Christ. Such a claim cannot be substantiated from the New Testament.

Worship in the New Testament Church

As I stated earlier, the book of Acts is not a worship manual. Luke did not see it necessary to outline a number of steps involved in an ordinary worship service in the first century or to prescribe what is to be worn, what a sanctuary is to look like, or any of the specifics of worship that one finds commanded in the Old Testament. There is no book of Leviticus for the New Testament church. Despite this lack of explicit command and extensive illustration of the nature of worship, there are several elements of early Christian worship which can be seen in the book of Acts as well as the New Testament epistles. There are several aspects of first-century Christian worship which are liturgical in nature.[38]

One of the most important considerations in evaluating early Christian worship is the nature of Jewish worship in the first century.[39] Between the Old and the New Testaments, the institution known as the synagogue was created, specifically as a place to worship for Jews who were outside of Jerusalem, and thus unable to be present at the temple. The synagogue had its own particular liturgy in the first century, and early Christians first worshipped within that Jewish context. Early Christian worship, as explained in the book of Acts, is essentially an

---

[38] See Jungmann, *The Early Liturgy*, 10–38, and Hurtado, *At the Origins*.
[39] See Senn, *Christian Liturgy*.

outgrowth of first-century Jewish worship patterns. Thus, if the Jewish service was a liturgical one, so were early Christian worship services.

Though there is no extensive first-century Jewish manual of worship, several elements of a traditional synagogue service can be roughly pieced together through a number of documents from around the first century.[40] During each service, there were at least two Scripture readings appointed for a variety of occasions. One reading came from the prophets and the other from the Torah. Some type of explanation and exposition of the text was given. The services also included some specific prayers, such as the *Kaddish*, that were used by the congregation at each service. The recitation of the *Shema*, which is essentially a basic creed about the identity of God, was normative in synagogue worship and in an individual's own personal life of worship. A prayer known as the *Tefilla* was prayed three times daily by worshippers of Yahweh and was also used in corporate worship. Finally, a priestly blessing was an important aspect of worship; this blessing is reflected in the benediction in modern Christian liturgy. All of these details demonstrate that the background in which Christian worship developed was a liturgical one.

The continuity between Jewish liturgical worship and Christian worship is attested in the book of Acts. In Acts 2, the worship of the early church is described as consisting in the breaking of bread (Holy Communion) [41] and "the prayers" (Acts 2:42). Some translations, unfortunately, do not include the article and simply read "prayers." This difference is significant, because Luke is not just referencing the practice of prayers in general, but of *the* prayers. These are specific prayers which are being prayed, and most likely, either the traditional Jewish prayers or a modified Christian form of those prayers. The point here is that the early Christians, when gathering together, had specific prayers which would be prayed at each meeting.

Along with specific prayers, the Jews had particular hours in each day when they would pray. Psalm 119, for example, mentions that there are seven times a day when prayers are offered (Psalm 119:164). The apostles Peter and John are said to go to the temple at the ninth hour, which is described as the "hour of prayer" (Acts 3:1). There is a consistent pattern of Christians since this time setting aside specific times during

---

[40] See Grabbe, *First Century Judaism*.
[41] Arthur Just's work on the Eucharist in the New Testament is helpful here in connecting Luke and Acts; see Just, *The Ongoing Feast*.

the day to pray certain prayers. The most common examples today are Matins (morning) and Vespers (evening) services. This pattern can also be practiced privately or with one's family as one develops a habit of family worship and prayer.

The Jewish calendar remained an essential part of the life of faith for early Christians. They measured time in light of the Jewish holy days throughout the year. For example, Luke mentions that he and Paul sailed away from Philippi "after the days of Unleavened Bread" (Acts 20:6). When writing to the Corinthians, Paul also mentions that he is going to stay in Ephesus "until Pentecost" (1 Cor. 16:8). The Jews' newfound faith in Christ did not result in the abandonment of the traditional Jewish calendar. Certainly, the meaning of each of these holy days had now changed due to the coming of Christ, and the apostles no longer participated in those ceremonies which were merely foreshadowing what was to come. The Jewish holy days were gradually transformed, so that Pentecost became the celebration of the Spirit's work at that time, and Passover was identified with Christ's death and resurrection.

These facts demonstrate that early Christians functioned on holy time. They had specific times each day set aside for prayer, they followed a calendar of holy days, and they also set aside one day each week for the worship of God. Though God does not set the same strict rules around Sunday that he did on the Jewish Sabbath, God gave the early Christians one particular day in which they were called to worship. Luke mentions that the church met on the first day of each week to break bread with one another (Acts 20:7). The apostle John refers to this day of the week as the "Lord's Day" (Rev. 1:10). In Acts, it is clear that every time the church met, Holy Communion was celebrated. For the Jews, Passover was celebrated one time each year. In the early church, the paschal liturgy was transferred from Passover to each Sunday. The liturgical service is generally divided up into two primary sections: the Service of the Word and the Service of the Sacrament. The Service of the Word largely arises from synagogue practice and prayers, and the Communion liturgy is based on Jewish Pentecost liturgy.

A further element of liturgical worship in the New Testament is the development of creedal statements. Many scholars argue that there are several phrases used in the New Testament which are aspects of early Christian liturgy, as either hymnody or early confessions of faith.[42]

---

[42] Hurtado, *Origins of Christian Worship*, 86–92.

Some early confessions of faith can be found in texts such as 1 Corinthians 8:6, 1 Corinthians 15:3-5, and Titus 3:4–7. The practice of making creeds comes from the Old Testament itself, which contains the *Shema*, the basis for Jewish creedal formulations and for the subsequent development of creeds in the Christian church. When Christians confess the Nicene, Apostles', or Athanasian creeds, they are continuing and developing this biblical aspect of Christian worship. Along with spoken creeds, the New Testament includes early hymns, such as in Philippians 2:6–11 and 1 Timothy 3:16. There are also several benedictions and doxologies included in the New Testament which were most likely used in worship services (Heb. 13:20–21, Jude 24-25, Eph. 3:20–21). The most well-known aspects of a liturgical service that arise out of the New Testament are those particular phrases which are connected to the administration of Holy Baptism and the Lord's Supper (Matt. 28:19, 1 Cor. 11:23–26). All of these texts demonstrate a liturgical structure in weekly worship at the time of the New Testament.

Conclusion

The use of liturgical worship is not a late innovation but is inherent within the worship practices explained in Scripture. The Old Testament contains very specific rubrics surrounding worship, including ceremonies, a calendar, repeated prayers, and clothing worn by priests. The New Testament explains worship both in heaven and in the early church. Heavenly worship includes repeated prayers, songs of praise, the wearing of robes, the use of candles and incense, bowing, and other liturgical elements. The New Testament church also worshipped in a formal manner, drawing upon common worship practices in first-century Judaism. This worship includes daily prayer, early creeds, doxologies, benedictions, multiple Scripture readings, and weekly Communion.

The New Testament does not give an extensive order of service to be used by the church, though it does give general outlines of what is to be present in a worship service. The church cannot, then, bind congregations to follow one specific form of liturgy. This is why churches in different countries and traditions have independently developed their own liturgies, which, though different, contain the same essential elements. What is clear, however, is that God intended his church to have a structured and formal mode of worship, which in the modern church would be considered liturgical.

CHAPTER 3:

ENTRANCE RITES

Every worship service or other event has a beginning. How the event begins is going to set the mood and theme of what is to come. For example, each of the *Star Wars* films begins with the phrase, "A long time ago in a galaxy far, far away...," which is then followed by the scrolling words *Star Wars* in space along with a crawl to explain the background of that particular film. As a fan of the franchise, when a new *Star Wars* film is released, I always attend the opening showing. The audience always breaks out into applause as these words appear on the screen, because this signals the beginning of the movie that the moviegoers are all looking forward to watching. How one of the films begins signals that this is a film in the *Star Wars* franchise. It sets a number of expectations and a specific mood for the following two-hour story. Likewise, every worship service has some kind of beginning rite. This is an essential aspect of the service because it sets the mood and tone for what is to come.

In some congregations, the beginning of the service is marked by a pastor welcoming the congregants and a praise band performing. While these churches likely do not think about these actions as an "entrance rite," they do signal to the people that the service is starting. The way the service begins implies something about the purpose, direction, and mood of the rest of the service. Contrastingly, in a liturgical service, the entrance rite includes three particular elements: an opening hymn, a processional, and an invocation.

The Opening Hymn
While many contemporary churches compile all of the songs into one "praise and worship" session at the beginning of the service, liturgical churches intersperse their songs throughout. The first hymn, known as the "opening hymn," is the first element of the liturgical worship service. Other hymns are sung before the sermon and following the benediction. There is often a selection of hymns sung during the distribution of Holy

Communion as well. All hymns are chosen based on the time in the church year and are connected to the theme of the sermon and lectionary readings. The opening hymn signals the time of transition when the people of God recognize that they are leaving ordinary life and entering into the presence of God as heaven and earth join together. The congregation stands during the opening hymn to honor God with their bodies; standing recognizes the holy event in which the people are partaking.

The Procession
As the opening hymn is sung, the pastor, along with those who are helping out during the worship service, process into the sanctuary. The procession usually includes an acolyte who is dressed in a white alb, lectors (readers), and assisting ministers and communion assistants. At times, the church choir may also process. The procession of the pastor signifies the people of God gathering together and moving toward the altar, where God meets his people. The altar is the focal point of the sanctuary, and thus the attention is drawn from the back of the church to the front, where the altar is.

One common element in worship that is associated with the procession is a processional cross. This is a cross on a long pole which is held up before the people of God as it is carried forward. The person who carries the cross is known as a crucifer, and he leads the procession ahead of pastors, acolytes, and others. The reason the cross takes this position is that the cross is at the center of the worship life of the church. The church lives under the cross, and the sacrificial death of Christ is the central message of the church. Thus, the cross goes forward first because the cross is where worship begins, and it is only through Christ's atoning death that sinners can gather to worship before the throne of God. The cross is carried forward to the chancel and is placed on a stand, where it remains for the remainder of the worship service. While the cross is being carried, the congregation faces it as it moves from the back of the sanctuary to the chancel. This action of the congregation is done not to honor the crucifer or the pastor, but to honor the work of Christ. As the cross moves toward the altar, so do the hearts of the people as they turn toward the chancel.

The use of a processional cross extends back at least to the sixth century, at which time historical records demonstrate that crosses were used in most congregations. They must have been used prior to that time, but there is no specific record of when they become common. When processional crosses were first introduced, they were brought forward and placed onto the altar. Through the centuries, two different crosses came to be used, and now most congregations have a separate altar cross. Like the processional cross, the placement of the cross on the altar again demonstrates the primacy of Christ's atoning death in Christian worship. Christ's atonement is the central proclamation of the church. Many congregations today also have a cross on the wall behind the altar.

When approaching the altar at the end of the procession, the pastor and others who have walked forward bow before the altar. This is done in reverence to Christ. To some, it may appear as if these people are adoring the altar itself, perhaps even in an idolatrous manner. The reverence, however, is paid not to the wood that makes up the altar but to the God who is present there. The altar is the connecting point between heaven and earth. It is where Christ makes his presence known as his true body and blood are brought down from heaven to earth under the forms of bread and wine. Since entrance into worship is entrance into the very presence of Christ, earthly worshippers bow just as do those heavenly beings before the throne of the Lamb.

As on the heavenly altar, candles are present either on the altar or to the side of the altar. The traditional Lutheran and Anglican practice was to have two candles at the back of the altar, but many churches have a larger number of candles following the Roman practice. The presence of candles in worship is a reflection of the candles described in Revelation as part of the holy sanctuary in heaven. The acolyte lights the candles on the altar following the procession as a symbol of the presence of Christ among the people of God in the worshipping community. These candles remain lit until the end of the service, when the acolyte extinguishes the altar candles and processes out of the sanctuary.

There is an additional candle known as the paschal candle which stands apart from the altar. This large candle symbolizes the eternal presence of Christ and is lit during Easter and on other special occasions during the church year.

The Invocation

Arguably, the most important part of the beginning of each worship service is the invocation. The invocation involves the pastor's reciting the name of the Triune God while he faces the congregation. Along with the words, "In the name of the Father and of the Son and of the Holy

Spirit," the sign of the cross is often made. This invocation is an announcement of the identity of the God who is present and who is being worshipped by the congregation.

Invocations of one kind or another are common in any sort of worship service, whether Christian or not. In some pagan religions, some specific incantation or prayer is to be said in order to invoke a given deity to appear. One must summon the being who is worshipped. We must not think of Christian worship in that manner. The invocation is not some kind of human verbal formula to entice God to be present with his people on Sunday morning. It is instead an *announcement*. God makes himself present in the congregation by his own will and power. There is nothing that the human creature can do to bring God down to earth. God comes freely.

In some congregations, pastors begin their worship service by saying, "We make our beginning in the name of the Father and of the Son and of the Holy Spirit." Though there is usually no ill intent when a pastor uses this formula, the words are imprecise and confuse the nature of worship. The pastor and the congregation do not "make their beginning" in the name of anything, because it is not the human creature that begins the worship service at all. Instead, it is God who begins the worship service.

One must properly understand the direction of worship, which is always heaven-to-earthward. God takes the initiative in human salvation, and he does the same in the context of human worship. Worship is about the divine presence and the gifts that God gives to sinners. The invocation reminds the congregation that the Triune God is the one who has brought the congregation together and who has united his people in one body. The role of the congregation is simply to receive God's gifts and then offer thanksgiving for the gifts received.

The Sign of the Cross
During the invocation, the pastor makes the sign of the cross over himself.[43] As a pastor, I find that there is often a misunderstanding of the nature and purpose of the sign of the cross in the Christian life, even

---

[43] Two great resources on the usefulness and history of the sign of the cross are Ghezzi, *Sign of the Cross*, and Andreopoulos, *Sign of the Cross*. The authors are Roman Catholic and Greek Orthodox respectively, and so some differences in worship and theology emerge in those texts. Their historical treatment, however, is greatly beneficial.

among those believers within Lutheran, Anglican, and other liturgical traditions. It is sometimes remarked by laity, for example, that the sign of the cross is something only the pastor does, and that it is probably just a holdover from Roman Catholic worship, with no practical value in the life of the average believer. Luther and other reformers, however, retained the use of the sign of the cross for a very particular reason. They saw it as a beneficial practice for both corporate worship and the individual life of prayer.

Christians have been making the sign of the cross since the church's earliest existence. In the first few centuries, it was usually done using the thumb on the forehead. This particular manner of crossing oneself still remains in baptisms as well as in the placing of ashes on one's forehead on Ash Wednesday. Making the sign of the cross was a way that God's people marked themselves as belonging to Christ. In a predominantly pagan society, making this sign was a way that believers in Rome were able to mark themselves as of a different faith than those of the world around them. Much like the popular *ichthus* (often called the "Jesus fish"), the sign of the cross was a means to identify the followers of Christ in the early church.

Eventually, the cross was made over the whole body in the manner that it is usually done today. Sometimes it was done using two fingers, but eventually, in Eastern countries it became standard to use three fingers when crossing oneself. The reason three fingers are used is because of the three persons of the Holy Trinity. In the West, the whole hand is often used, and the five fingers represent the five wounds of Christ. The sign of the cross remains in Eastern Orthodox, Roman Catholic, Anglican, and Lutheran churches, though each of these traditions has a slightly different use of the sign of the cross.

The sign of the cross is not a superstition or empty ritual, but it is a powerful reminder of one's identity in Christ. This gesture is often performed while the words "Father, Son, and Holy Spirit" are spoken, due to the connection between the cross and the Triune God. It is significant that these words are the same ones that the pastor pronounces over a person who is being baptized. Along with the application of water and the Triune name, the sign of the cross is often made by the pastor on the head and heart of the one receiving the sacrament. When we make the sign of the cross, we are remembering our baptisms. This is a way Christians remind themselves that they are God's baptized people. They have been baptized into the name of the Triune God, and they belong to the Triune God. This symbol is a reminder to us of who we are in Christ, and it can even serve as a wordless prayer.

Making the sign of the cross during the invocation is a reminder that the service presently beginning involves the fellowship of the baptized. Those who have received the sacrament of baptism unite together in worship and praise the God in whose name they have been adopted. In some congregations, there is a tradition of dipping one's hand in water and making the sign of the cross upon entering into the sanctuary. This action further serves to remind believers of their baptisms, where they were united to Christ and God removed their guilt.

Conclusion

Entrance rites, like the rest of the service, will vary depending upon the congregation. Some churches have elaborate processionals, and others do not. Despite whatever differences of practice exist, it is important that the beginning of the service is centered in what *God* is doing rather than what the congregation does. As worship begins, heaven and earth become one as the Triune God condescends to his people in the Divine Service.

CHAPTER 4:
CONFESSION and ABSOLUTION

Following the invocation, the congregation recognizes that it has entered into the presence of the holy Triune God. Consequently, the wickedness of those gathering is exposed. In the light of God's purity, our impurities are clear before our eyes. We sinful people cannot stand before a holy, perfect God. Therefore, the congregation joins together to confess their sins before God. God responds with a cleansing that comes through the words of the absolution.

Isaiah in the Throne Room of God
The purpose of the confession is displayed in Isaiah's account of his divine call given in the throne room of God. The Lord took Isaiah from his earthly abode and brought him into God's own heavenly throne room. This is the occasion when Isaiah is called into the prophetic office. The significance of this event for the current study is that this is the clearest biblical description of what happens when one enters into the sanctuary of God. Isaiah's experience before the face of God mirrors the experience of every worshipper when entering the sanctuary.

In Isaiah's vision, God is described as having a kingly robe with a train so large that it fills the entire temple. This great Lord is worshipped continually by two seraphim who cry out that God is thrice holy. God's majesty is further portrayed by his booming voice, which is so loud that the entire temple shakes at his word. In view of the holiness on display, Isaiah cries out in despair:

> Woe is me, for I am undone!
> Because I am a man of unclean lips,
> And I dwell in the midst of a people of unclean lips;
> For my eyes have seen the King,
> The LORD of hosts. (Is. 6:5)

Isaiah's vision of God immediately leads to a recognition of his personal uncleanness, which then leads to a confession of sin on behalf of both himself and the worshipping community.

The Presence of God Brings Death to the Unholy

Though Isaiah survives his experience in the presence of the Triune God, there are several instances in Scripture wherein other people are not so fortunate. One such example is that of Uzzah (2 Sam. 6:6–8). After David's anointing as king over Israel and a subsequent defeat of the Philistine army, the king led the Jewish people in a musical procession as they carried the ark to the city of Jerusalem. The ark had been placed on a new cart, and at one point during the procession, the oxen began to stumble, allowing the possibility of the ark's falling to the ground. In response to this event, Uzzah stretched out his hand in order to keep the ark from falling onto the ground. He was immediately struck dead.

God's actions in this narrative might seem odd in light of the usual perception of God which many Christians have. In fact, David himself did not understand God's actions and protested the taking of this man's life. What is essential to understand about this story is that it demonstrates the holiness of God and the unholiness of the sinful human creature. The ark was the holiest place in all of Israel. It was where God's presence dwelt in a special way for the people. God is pure, and thus the place of his presence must also be pure. If a holy God touches an unclean thing, that unclean thing must be destroyed.

While the ark began to fall off the cart, Uzzah had two options: either he could let the ark fall onto the dirt, or he could stretch out his hand and catch it. As most of us probably would, Uzzah assumed that his hand was cleaner than the dirt. This assumption was wrong. The dirt, in and of itself, is not unholy. The ground, though affected by sin, is not itself sinful. The earth has not acted against God's holy will in rebellion against him. The same cannot be said of humanity. Unlike the land, Uzzah was a rebellious creature; he was infected with sin and uncleanness. Spiritually, apart from Christ, we are all, like Uzzah, unclean.

The concept that God's presence brings death to sinners is explained in several other places in Scripture. During the time of the Exodus, the Israelites feared God's wrath due to his presence in the tabernacle. The people cried to Moses, "Surely we die, we perish, we all perish! Whoever even comes near the tabernacle of the LORD must die. Shall we all utterly die?" (Num. 17:12–13). This was not an unfounded concern; God himself had said to Moses, "No man shall see Me, and live" (Ex. 33:20). As is described in the beginning of Genesis, death is the result of sin before a holy God, and all have sinned (Rom. 3:23). Therefore, it is natural for any sinner to fear the presence of God in his holiness and majesty.

The Confession of Sins

The invocation is the announcement that the Triune God is present in the worshipping community. Heaven and earth have joined together, and as Isaiah did, we have entered into the very throne room of God in the heavenly sanctuary. Like Isaiah, we recognize that we are unholy when entering into God's presence. God's majesty reveals the sin which exists within us. We cry unto God, "Woe is me!" as we recognize our unworthiness in the divine presence. This recognition of sin is both individual and corporate. We each confess sins with our own individual voices, but we speak that confession with the whole church.

There are several different forms of the traditional confession of sins. These confessions follow the same general pattern in expressing the expansive nature of sin within the Christian's life. Sin is confessed in "thought, word, and deed." Sin does not refer only to the outward actions of a person, or even just to one's words. Sin is so expansive that it extends throughout one's daily thought life. There is no one in a Christian congregation who cannot confess to have sinned in this threefold manner. Sin is expressed also in terms of what *has* been done and what has *not* been done. One should think not simply about outward actions that appear sinful, but also about even the various missed opportunities to serve one's neighbor. Along with confessing sins, one recognizes that sin deserves death, both temporal and eternal.

A time of private and silent confession occurs prior to the public confession of sins. This time allows the penitent sinner to think through the various struggles which have occurred within the past week before speaking out loud. The words should not be an empty ritual, but specific sins should be repented of as one confesses with the congregation.

In some churches, there is no single confession and absolution that is used. In order to encourage variation in the worship service, different confessions will be used each week in accord with the theme of that particular service. The intent is to ensure that one thinks about what is spoken rather than simply repeating a memorized formula. While the motive behind this is an admirable one, there are two problems with straying from one consistent confession of sins. First, the use of different words each week will not necessarily cause one to think more meaningfully about those words. It might be the case that the individual actually cannot focus as well, because rather than thinking through words which are known, the person may be focusing solely on reading the new confession correctly. Second, and more importantly, newer confessions of sin are usually not universal in scope but focus on only one particular aspect of sin that is in accord with the theme of that service. This may (1) cause worshippers to confess sins that they do not actually struggle with, or (2) leave them without the chance to confess the sins they *have* committed that week. Much like the traditional wedding vows, the historic words have lasted so long and have been used so universally because they are so extensive. Nothing as articulate and concise has been written since.

Cleansing Follows a Recognition of Sin
The story of Isaiah's experience in the throne room of God does not end with the death of sinful Isaiah before the holiness of God. Instead, the narrative speaks about an act of cleansing. Following Isaiah's confession of both individual and corporate uncleanness, God performs a sacramental act to purify Isaiah. An angel is sent by God as an instrument of grace to the sinful prophet. The angel carries a hot coal with tongs and places the coal on Isaiah's lips. Then the angel cries:

> Behold, this has touched your lips;
> Your iniquity is taken away,
> And your sin purged. (Is. 6:7)

God's response to the sins of believers is not to punish, but to bring cleansing. The human minister serves the same role as this angel in Isaiah's vision: he is an instrument to bring healing to God's unclean people. The words of absolution then serve as a means of grace just as did the burning coal for Isaiah. God does not bring forgiveness in a vacuum, but through specific means directed toward individual believers.

The Old Testament includes a number of cleansing rituals prior to various acts of worship. Before God appeared to the people of Israel at Mt. Sinai, he called the Israelites, through Moses, to sanctify themselves. They washed their garments, recognizing that to touch God's holy mountain meant death (Ex. 19:10–14). Thus, some type of cleansing in the presence of God was symbolized, though the people were still unable to approach God's holiness without harm. The priests, who *were* able to approach God, similarly had to cleanse themselves (Ex. 19:22). There were several ongoing rituals in Israel similar to these events at Mt. Sinai, such as the vesting of the priests. Before putting on their holy garments, the Levitical priests were required to thoroughly wash their bodies (Lev. 16:4). Ritual washings were connected with offerings, as well as with the release of the scapegoat (Lev. 16:24–28). All of these cleansing rituals signify the necessity of an act of consecration and forgiveness for one to enter into the presence of Yahweh without facing death.

The New Testament Basis of Confession and Absolution

Forgiveness is a central theme in the New Testament. It is spoken of in a general sense, in which, by Christ's vicarious death, forgiveness has been won for all people (Rom. 5:18). This concept is what theologians refer to as objective justification. This objective forgiveness which Christ won must, however, be applied to the individual and received in faith. God delivers this pronouncement of justification through the means of grace: Word and Sacrament.

One of the most popular passages connected to forgiveness is 1 John 1:9, wherein John promises that when sins are confessed unto God, "He is faithful and just to forgive us our sins and to cleanse us from all unrighteousness." God gives his people confidence that genuine confession of sins always leads to the assurance of pardon. One might assume from this text, however, that God simply wants to hear a confession of sins in private prayer rather than in a public worship setting. Other places in the New Testament make it apparent that confession of sins is something which should also be done among other believers. In James, for example, we are told that Christians should confess their sins before one another (James 5:16). Though this text is not necessarily a reference to a public worship service, a corporate confession is one manner in which the apostle's injunction may be carried out.

The primary basis for the liturgical practice of confession and absolution is a selection of texts from the gospels in which Jesus gives the keys of the kingdom of heaven to his apostles; through this act, the apostles are granted the ability to forgive and retain sins. The clearest of such texts is from one of the first resurrection appearances, described in John 20. In this text, Jesus breathes his Holy Spirit upon the disciples and says to them, "If you forgive the sins of any, they are forgiven them; if you retain the sins of any, they are retained" (John 20:23). This is not simply a declaration of Christ that the apostles are to proclaim that forgiveness is available in Christ. Instead, the apostles are given the authority to *actually forgive sins*. Pastors serve, as did the apostles, in this role. They deliver the gospel to those who confess, and in doing so, they forgive sins in the stead of Christ. This is why, in many Lutheran liturgies, the absolution contains the words, "I forgive you." This forgiveness is not dependent upon any special quality of the pastor, but on the word of Christ who speaks through the mouth of the minister.

The two other texts related to the pastor's ability to forgive the sins of the penitent are from the Gospel of Matthew. In Matthew 16, St. Peter, the head of the apostles, confesses that Jesus is the Christ. Following this confession, Jesus says to Peter,

> "[Y]ou are Peter, and on this rock I will build My church, and the gates of Hades shall not prevail against it. And I will give you the keys of the kingdom of heaven, and whatever you bind on earth will be bound in heaven, and whatever you loose on earth will be loosed in heaven." (Matt. 16:18–19)

This text has unfortunately been used for many centuries as a definitive proof for the validity of the papacy in the line of St. Peter. That is not, however, the intended meaning of the text. Rather, Jesus speaks about the rock upon which the church is built: the confession of Jesus as the Christ. Peter, as the chief apostle, makes this confession, and Jesus then grants to him the keys of binding and loosing sins. This gift is given not only to Peter, but to the entire church, as is expressed in Matthew 18:18. It is the *church* which has the keys of the kingdom of heaven, and consequently, the authority to forgive and retain sins.

The pastor has no indelible character placed upon him so that he might forgive and retain sins on account of anything within him. Instead, the power to forgive sins is given to the entire church; the pastor is the one placed in the position to exercise those keys, and he does this through both the proclamation of absolution and the retaining of sins through church discipline. He does not speak on his own authority, but in the stead of Christ and through the authority of the church.

Private Confession and Absolution
Along with corporate confession and absolution, the use of private confession is available in many congregations, especially within the

Lutheran tradition. The Roman tradition includes within the rite of private confession a number of penances which are to be performed by the penitent in response to whatever sins are confessed. This idea of performing penances has been rejected by Christians who come from the Reformation tradition as affront to the gospel. Christ's atonement is the only satisfaction needed for sins, and thus penance is unnecessary and burdens consciences. In Article XXV of the Augsburg Confession, the early Lutheran reformers argued that, while the medieval church abused private confession, the practice itself "is retained among us both because of the great benefit of absolution and because of other advantages for consciences" (AC XXV.13). Following the Augsburg Confession, many Lutheran pastors today continue to offer private absolution.

The practice of private confession and absolution seems to have become formalized in the early Middle Ages around the time of Gregory the Great (circa AD 600). This practice appears to have arisen around specific grave sins which needed to be confessed by certain congregants, but it eventually became standard for all Christians, who were required to confess all sins to a priest on a regular basis. The imposition of confession as a divine mandate became harmful to burdened consciences and confused human works with Christ's atonement. Instead of being a chance to receive absolution in the context of pastoral care, confession became an unbearable burden wherein one had to remember all sins, a requirement that is directly opposed to the scriptural teaching that such a thing is impossible (Ps. 19:12).

In the Lutheran tradition, private confession and absolution is offered within the context of pastoral care for a burdened conscience. When a believer is doubting the forgiveness of a particular sin, the confessional serves as a way in which the penitent can hear absolution for that sin. The pastor is, in this context, employing the keys of the kingdom that he has been granted by Christ so that one may be assured of one's standing in Christ. There is no mandate that congregants *must* go to private confession and absolution, but it is encouraged.

The Retaining of Sins

A topic which is often avoided in discussions of absolution, but which is an unfortunate necessity, is the retaining of sins. When Jesus grants the keys of the kingdom to the apostles in both Matthew 16 and John 20, he mentions both aspects of the church's duty: ministers are to forgive and to retain sins.

Church discipline is an unfortunate necessity in a fallen world. While pastors are called to proclaim forgiveness to all who are penitent, it must be recognized that there are unrepentant people within the visible church, and there will be until the eschaton (Matt. 13:24–30). Though ministers not called to search the hearts of each congregant in order to determine that person's spiritual state, excommunication should be exercised in the case of unrepentant, open sin. This task should never be taken lightly, and a number of steps should be taken prior to excommunication in order to encourage repentance (Matt. 18:15–19). When someone refuses to listen, however, such a person is to be expelled from Holy Communion and considered an unbeliever (1 Cor. 5:5). Excommunication is never simply for the purpose of punishing sin but has repentance as its ultimate goal. When one who is under discipline repents, that person is to be immediately received back into the fellowship as a brother or sister.

This is an important point to understand when speaking about both public and private absolution. When an unrepentant sinner is under church discipline, the words of absolution are not for that person. It is to be made clear that the proclamation of forgiveness is for only the *repentant* believer. This is not to say that one must have perfect repentance in order to receive absolution. Such a thing is completely impossible in a fallen world. Our repentance itself must be covered by the blood and righteousness of Christ due to our sinful nature, which hinders all good deeds. However, when one obstinately refuses repentance, such a one is to be excluded from the absolution until he or she comes back to a state of repentance. To fail to exercise church discipline is to give false assurance to unrepentant sinners and to disobey the command of Christ.

Liturgical Postures
During the confession and absolution, the pastor takes on two different liturgical postures. When the confession is read, the minister faces the altar; when the absolution is pronounced, the pastor faces the congregation. These postures are significant both theologically and practically. In his role as minister, the pastor has both a priestly and a prophetic function. A priest speaks to God on behalf of the people. This is why the priests in the Old Testament offered up sacrifices—in order to serve as mediators. Within the context of prayer, the pastor, serving as mediator, faces the altar, offering up prayers for and with the people of

the congregation. The role of a prophet, in contrast, is to proclaim the words and will of God to the people. This is the role of the pastor in reading Scripture and in preaching. Thus, when proclaiming God's Word to the people, the pastor faces the congregation.

These two postures recur throughout the worship service. Any time the pastor speaks to God, he faces the altar. When he speaks to the congregation, he faces the people. While speaking in a mode of prayer, the pastor will also often hold out his hands in the *orans* position,[44] which is a biblical posture for prayer (1 Tim. 2:8). The pastor's posture is instructive for the congregation, to make them aware of whether the pastor is praying or proclaiming at a given time.

---

[44] Meaning that the pastor holds up his hands.

CHAPTER 5:
INTROIT, KYRIE, and HYMN OF PRAISE

The introductory aspects of the worship service conclude after the pronouncement of God's absolution to the congregation. The baptized people of God have heard the announcement that the Triune God is present, they have confessed their sins, and they have received cleansing. Following the absolution, the Service of the Word begins with prayer and praise in preparation for the Scripture readings and sermon.

Introit

The first aspect of the worship service following the entrance rites is the singing or speaking of an introit, psalm, or hymn of praise. As addressed above, the Divine Service presents a continual pattern of the congregation's asking for mercy, God's granting mercy, and the people's responding with praise and thanksgiving. The introit is an instance of praise, wherein part of a psalm or another Scripture is used by the congregation to praise the God who has absolved them from sin.

The introit is usually taken from a psalm and is sung antiphonally. This means that during the introit, two different groups sing parts of the psalm. Most often, a pastor and congregation sing or speak responsively, but a choir or cantor might also sing. In the introit, an antiphon is added both before and after the psalm section which is used for that day. At times, the introit incorporates another portion of Scripture (those that do this are known as "irregular" introits) in accord with the particular theme of a given service. The introit changes each Sunday and aligns with the theme of the day along with the time of the church year. In some traditions, an entire psalm is used in each worship service, and in others, a hymn of praise is found in its place.

In the earliest liturgies, an entire psalm was used each week instead of the introit, which was introduced in the fifth century. Initially, the psalm was part of the entrance rite and was sung as the pastor and other helpers in the service processed to the altar. The word *introit* itself reflects this tradition; the word literally means "entrance." After the introduction of an opening hymn to the beginning section of worship, the psalm was moved to the place where it exists in the service today. Martin Luther argued that, rather than using the shorter introit, the church should reestablish the practice of using an entire psalm in the worship service. This is done today in some Anglican and Lutheran congregations, though the use of an introit is still more common.[45]

The singing of psalms in worship is an ancient tradition, extending back to the worship of Israel under the reign of David. God inspired these 150 songs to be used by his people in corporate worship. Though there are other songs in the Old Testament, the worship of Israel primarily consisted of these psalms. In the New Testament, the church continued the practice of singing psalms as a central aspect of worship. There was no necessity of changing the psalms for specifically Christian hymns since the psalms themselves are understood Christologically. The practice of singing psalms is referenced twice by Paul. He states that the Ephesians should be "speaking to one another in psalms and hymns and spiritual songs" (Eph. 5:19). A parallel passage in Colossians similarly notes, "Let the word of Christ dwell in you richly in all wisdom, teaching and admonishing one another in psalms and hymns and spiritual songs" (Col. 3:16). Along with Christian hymns, the Jewish Psalter was central in early Christian worship.

It is an unfortunate fact that in many contemporary churches, the psalms remain largely unknown. They are referenced simply as poetry rather than as hymns. It is common for a modern congregation to never sing psalms, while still often singing hymns which are based on particular sections of the Psalter. If the commands regarding worship in the New Testament have any value for the contemporary church, then worship *must* include psalms. This cannot be omitted. Unfortunately, even in contemporary churches which do utilize and value the psalms, the psalms are not used in the manner in which God gave them.

There are two primary ways in which the psalms are not used rightly in a worship service. First, the psalms are merely spoken. Certainly, it is more advisable for the psalms to be spoken than not to be used at all. They were not, however, given to be spoken. Every reference to the use of psalms in worship in Scripture denotes their being sung by worshippers. Second, some traditions, in their desire to sing psalms (sometimes exclusively), have reworked the language of the Psalter to fit the rhythm and tune of popular hymns. Though again, this is a better

---

[45] The introit is omitted altogether in most Anglican services.

option than not using the psalms at all, the congregation is singing a paraphrase rather than the actual words of Scripture. The ancient method of psalm-singing—through chanting—is the best means by which the congregation can use these hymns in worship. Chanting can be done antiphonally, so that both the pastor and the congregation (or choir) can sing. Also, one need not change the word order or construction of a psalm in order to make it fit a chant.

Following the psalm or introit, the congregation speaks or sings the *Gloria Patri*, which is a doxology to the Triune God. The *Gloria Patri* contains the words, "Glory be to the Father and to the Son and to the Holy Spirit; as it was in the beginning, is now, and shall be forever. Amen." This Trinitarian addendum is a reminder to the congregation that it is the Triune God who inspired the Psalter and to whom the congregation sings. The *Gloria Patri* also ensures that whatever the tone or message of the introit of that day is, it ends in the mode of praise. The *Gloria Patri* has been used at least since the mid-fourth century and echoes the various Trinitarian benedictions and doxologies used in Scripture (Rom. 16:27, Eph. 3:20–21, etc.).

Kyrie

The posture of the congregation moves at this point from praise to a request for mercy from God. In the *Kyrie*, God's people ask for his grace once again, recognizing the fact that it is only by mercy that any of their requests can be granted. The phrase *kyrie eleison* is Greek for "Lord have mercy." There are a variety of ways in which the *Kyrie* can be incorporated into the service, but the phrase "Lord have mercy" is always included.

The basic prayer "Lord have mercy" comes from the parable of the Pharisee and the tax collector in Luke 18:9–14. In this story, both of these men offer up prayers to God. The prayer of the Pharisee consists of his thanking God that he has been created better than others. In contrast to this, the tax collector cries out, "God, be merciful to me a sinner!" (Luke 18:13). The prayer of the tax collector, unlike that of the Pharisee, resulted in his justification. Because the tax collector recognized and admitted that he had no personal righteousness, God vindicated him for the sake of Christ. When praying the *Kyrie*, Christians recognize that they, like this tax collector, have no righteousness to offer God. Instead, they are beggars in need of divine mercy.

This prayer for divine mercy is not only a corporate confession of the church gathered in worship, but of each individual as he or she stands before God. This posture should accompany the Christian each day, as one is always in need of God's mercy. In the Eastern church, a form of the *Kyrie* known as the "Jesus Prayer" is used in personal devotion. This alternative version of a *Kyrie* contains the words, "Lord Jesus Christ, Son of God, have mercy on me the sinner." This phrase is often repeated in prayer and serves as a continual reminder of the reality of sin in the Christian life. No matter how sanctified one is, he or she is always in need of God's mercy for daily sustenance and spiritual life.

Though prayers like the *Kyrie* are as old as the New Testament, the introduction of this prayer into the corporate worship of the church is not apparent until the fourth century, and it soon became standard for both the Eastern and Western churches. In its earliest forms, the *Kyrie* includes a variety of petitions with "Lord have mercy" as a response. Since the time of the Reformation, it has been common to use a shorter form of the *Kyrie*, in which the congregation sings the threefold "Lord have mercy, Christ have mercy, Lord have mercy." Many churches have now restored the earlier and more historic form of the *Kyrie*, in which "Lord have mercy" is not a stand-alone prayer of the church but a response to a variety of petitions lifted up by the minister before God. At certain times, a hymn based upon the simple prayer "Lord, have mercy" is used in place of the traditional *Kyrie*. Whatever form this petition for mercy takes, it is a time when God's people turn to him in prayer following the praise given in the previous introit.

Hymn of Praise
When God's people ask for his mercy, his response ought not be doubted. He will always answer the cries of his people. In recognition of the mercy that God gives to his people in granting forgiveness and answering their previous petitions, the people of God once again offer thanks and praise in response to God's actions in behalf of the congregation. This is done with a song of praise.

The most common song of praise used in worship following the *Kyrie* is the *Gloria in Excelsis*, or "Glory be to God on high." This ancient hymn is taken from the Gospel of Luke, where the angels sing at the birth of Christ: "Glory to God in the highest, And on earth peace, goodwill toward men!" (Luke 2:14). In addition to these words, a threefold structure is used to praise the Father, Son, and Holy Spirit each in the same manner. All praise is Trinitarian in nature. By joining in the hymn of the angels, the church recognizes that in the Divine Service, heaven and earth are united; the church militant sings with the church triumphant as the entire host of heaven glorifies the Triune God. The *Gloria in Excelsis* first arose in the Eastern church and was introduced in the West in the sixth century. It was not commonly used in the Mass until the later Middle Ages. It has been standard in liturgical services since the time of the Reformation.

Other songs may at times be used in place of the traditional *Gloria*. A modern addition to the liturgy here is the song "This Is the Feast," which was written by musician Richard Hillert in 1978. Like the *Gloria in Excelsis*, this song has its roots in the worship of the angels as described in Scripture. The song follows the theme of the eschatological feast of the Lamb, in which all of God's people participate through the celebration of Holy Communion. In the sacrament, heaven and earth join as Christ's body and blood are received. The phrase "worthy is the Lamb who was slain" is used throughout the song, echoing the words of Revelation 5:13. The church should not be opposed to using new songs in this section of the service, provided such songs continue the theme of participation in the worship of Christ alongside of the angels and saints in eternal glory.

Collect of the Day
Each Sunday, a prayer called the collect of the day is used in the service following the hymn of praise. This prayer changes week after week, and it reflects the theme of the church year as well as the scriptural texts for that week. These prayers are repeated every one to three years, depending on which lectionary the congregation uses. These written prayers can be either spoken or chanted by the pastor, and the congregation responds with an "Amen."

Each collect has a very particular structure. The pastor begins with the customary greeting, "The Lord be with you," and the congregation responds, "And also with you" or "And with thy spirit." The prayer then begins with an address, which is almost always directed toward God the Father. One or more divine attributes are then mentioned which relate to the remainder of the prayer. There is then a petition, followed by a desired result of that petition. Finally, the prayer involves the name of Christ, who is invoked as the mediator through which the believer is able to approach the Father in prayer.

In this section of the liturgy, the pastor returns to his priestly role as he leads the congregation in prayer following its offering of praise to the Triune God. The collect of the day serves as a transition point from the time of praise and petition to the time for Scripture readings and ultimately, the sermon.

The use of a collect following the hymn of praise is a distinctively Western tradition. It is used in Lutheran, Anglican, Roman Catholic, and some other liturgical churches. It has never been standard in Eastern Orthodox or Coptic worship.

CHAPTER 6:
SCRIPTURE READINGS

Though every aspect of the worship service that follows the confession and absolution until the celebration of Holy Communion is technically part of the Service of the Word, the most specific Word-centric aspect of the Divine Service consists of the three Scripture readings as well as the proclamation of God's Word in the pulpit.

In this section of the service, the pastor takes on a prophetic role. He brings the Word of God to the congregation and thus faces the congregation while speaking. The emphasis moves from the altar, where praise is offered, to the lectern, where Scripture is read. The dialogue changes from man-to-God to God-to-man. In his Word, God acts through both law and gospel as his people are convicted of sins and made new by the Spirit, who is always present through the proclamation of the divine Word. The people are also encouraged unto holy living and acts of love within the world that God has placed them into.

As early as there is record, Christians have emphasized the reading of Scripture in worship. This focus is not original in the Christian church but echoes the nature of synagogue worship, where a variety of readings were used, usually including one text from the Pentateuch as well as one from a prophetic book or psalm. The New Testament epistles themselves were written to be read in front of congregations. Thus, the New Testament was written that it might be publicly proclaimed to the church. In today's culture, books are easily accessible, and there is an extremely high literacy rate. Due to that fact, modern Christians are tempted to see the Bible as a private book to be used in personal devotion. While reading the Bible privately is certainly to be encouraged, God gave it primarily for the purpose of the corporate gathering of his people.

Throughout Christian history, and in different regions of the church, a variety of practices surrounding these Scripture readings have arisen. In the earliest Christian settings, the Old Testament had a prominent position as the New Testament books were being written and circulated. Eventually, the New Testament readings became more prominent than the Old. During the Middle Ages, the Old Testament reading was omitted altogether, and the church had both a gospel and epistle lesson each service. The Eastern Orthodox tradition continues this practice of not including an Old Testament reading in Sunday or daily lectionaries.[46] The Coptic Orthodox church has the most Scripture readings, with eight in each service, along with a separate reading honoring the life of a saint. In contemporary Western churches, the service includes an Old Testament lesson, an epistle reading, a gospel reading, and an appointed psalm.

Types of Lectionaries
The earliest lectionaries were used in synagogues. Though it is not clear that there was a strict daily or weekly lectionary, there were certain readings tied to specific holy days throughout the year. The practice of appointing certain readings for certain days eventually grew, and readings become standardized in both Judaism and Christianity.

In early Christianity, the practice of assigning readings to holy days was adopted from Judaism. In different regions of the church, more elaborate lectionaries were created, though the use of readings remained rather free. It was common for ministers to preach through a whole book (this practice is called *lectio continua*); such was the practice of the famous preacher John Chrysostom. By the early Middle Ages, at least by the time of Charlemagne (circa AD 800), there was a standard set of readings for each Sunday of the church year, with collects that accorded to those readings. These readings went through a one-year cycle and thus were repeated on the same days each year. Under this practice, the entirety of the New Testament was not read throughout the year, but all major teachings were covered.

During the time of the Reformation, the use of lectionaries was retained in the Lutheran and Anglican traditions. There were, at times, some slight modifications of the contemporary lectionaries by Luther and others for particular theological reasons. The Lutheran and Anglican traditions both significantly decreased the number of holy days throughout the year, especially as related to extrabiblical saints. For that reason, readings that might have been tied to those feasts were changed.

The readings in the gospels generally follow the broader pattern of Christ's life as explained throughout the church year. The year begins with Advent, with readings that emphasize the coming of the Messiah,

---

[46] However, Old Testament readings are used on certain Feast Days.

culminating in the celebration of Christ's birth on Christmas as the Lucan nativity narrative is read. Following Christmas, the lectionary follows the events of Christ's life, including his circumcision, teaching in the temple, baptism, and so on. The events of the last days of Christ's life are read during Lent, and especially in Holy Week. Christ's death is remembered on Good Friday as the Passion narrative is read, and then the story of the resurrection is read on Easter Sunday. Following Easter are readings on Christ's ascension as well as Pentecost. The second half of the church year emphasizes Christ's teachings rather than his acts. The readings, and consequently sermons, focus on Christ's parables and spoken messages.

In recent years, there has been a departure from the traditional one-year lectionary for a three-year cycle. Following the second Vatican Council (1962–1965), the Roman Catholic Church opted for a new lectionary which followed an A, B, and C set of readings. Year A is based primarily on the Gospel of Matthew; year B focuses on Mark; year C emphasizes readings from Luke. The Gospel of John is interspersed throughout each of these cycles. The goal of this new lectionary was to expand the knowledge of Scripture among the laity and give a greater range of texts for preaching.

A number of Protestant groups, following Vatican II, adopted a three-year lectionary. The Revised Common Lectionary (1994) is used by a variety of Protestant groups including Lutherans, Anglicans, Methodists, and Presbyterians. This is the most common lectionary now used within Protestantism, and thus the three-year cycle is the most common type of lectionary in Western Christianity.

There are a number of benefits to using a three-year lectionary which have been emphasized by those who have adopted it. First, it broadens a congregation's knowledge of Scripture. Second, it allows for an emphasis on each gospel distinctively instead of mixing them together. Third, it helps preaching, as pastors now have a larger variety of texts to preach from. Fourth, it emphasizes unity within the church as this is now the most common set of readings. These benefits have caused most Lutherans to switch to a three-year cycle, with some caveats. The Lutheran Church—Missouri Synod has a lectionary cycle which is slightly different from the Revised Common Lectionary. The reason for these alterations is to emphasize different aspects of the gospel reading in using different Old Testament or epistle lessons. There are a number of theological implications to the selection of Old Testament lessons in connection to the gospel readings.[47] Also, some Lutherans have resisted this change and prefer to continue using the one-year cycle as has been used for many centuries. Since God has not commanded a particular lectionary to be used in worship, this is an area of Christian freedom, wherein congregations can freely differ with one another regarding which lectionary is read.

Benefits of Using a Lectionary
There are several benefits to a church's adopting a historic lectionary rather than simply allowing the pastor to preach on whatever text he desires each week. These benefits include a greater emphasis on the reading of Scripture, on the connection between the Old and New Testaments, and on the catholicity of the church, as well as the avoidance of topical sermons.

In non-liturgical congregations, it is common to have only one Scripture reading during the service. This Scripture reading is selected based on the sermon and reflects the theme of that morning's message. Often, a pastor will preach on a very small portion of text (sometimes just a couple of verses), and thus that small section of Scripture is all one hears on a given Sunday. The lectionary ensures that this issue will be avoided in two ways. First, the selections chosen each week are always more than a few verses. The congregation will always, therefore, hear the context of the verses that are preached on rather than one isolated verse. Second, the lectionary ensures that the congregation hears at least three Scripture readings each week, alongside of the Scripture that is contained in the rest of the liturgy and hymnody. Even if the pastor has a bad Sunday and his sermon is unbiblical, the Scripture itself will still be proclaimed in the liturgy.

Another problem in some contemporary forms of Evangelicalism is a lack of understanding of the Old Testament. In certain traditions, it is taught that the Old Testament is all about national promises given to the physical nation of Israel, and the New Testament is about the church. The Old and New Testaments are two totally separate covenants, and

---

[47] For example, the Roman Church has a particular emphasis on Mary as the fulfillment of the ark of the covenant. Thus, in the Roman tradition, it might be natural to connect a gospel reading about Mary with an Old Testament text about the ark of the covenant. Since such a connection is not often made within the Protestant tradition, a different Old Testament text may be appointed.

thus the Old Testament is largely irrelevant to the church. A large portion of Christians are ignorant of the Old Testament, and specifically of its relationship to the New Testament. In the lectionary, the Old Testament readings are chosen in accord with the gospel. There are similar themes used in both readings, and sometimes the Old Testament lesson is explicitly cited either in the gospel or epistle reading. These connections help the congregation to understand the Christological focus of the Old Testament. The connections also give the pastor an opportunity to tie the themes of each reading together and explain how the Old Testament, epistle, and gospel lessons are unified.

The lectionary is a great benefit to the pastor when he is preparing sermons to be given on Sunday mornings. He is bound not to his own thoughts or desires but to the text that is given to him. Every pastor, no matter how balanced he may be, has certain biblical and theological issues that he enjoys studying and speaking about more than others. Consequently, when a pastor is able to pick his own texts for worship, it is likely that whatever topic he is most interested in becomes a continual sermon theme. The lectionary helps pastors to be balanced in their preaching. It also gives them specific texts to preach on so that they don't just preach topical sermons that pull together many disconnected texts. A final help to the pastor is that the lectionary causes him to look at a larger portion of a text when preaching. Often, pastors choose to preach on just two or three verses at a time, and while doing that, they miss the context of that Scripture and misread it.

Finally, the lectionary emphasizes that each congregation is not autonomous, but all Christians are part of the church universal. Each congregation does not simply have its own disconnected service but uses the same liturgy and readings as millions of other Christians throughout the world. This unity can serve as a great help to pastors, who can consult with other pastors while preparing a sermon. They can give one another aids and advice as they study the same text together. The lectionary also aids in Christian fellowship, as friends and family members who go to different churches in various locations can speak together about the readings for that week.

Though at most times, it is the best practice to follow the lectionary readings, these should not be viewed as a straightjacket for preaching. Each pastor is called to his own unique congregation and knows the particular needs of that congregation. There may be particular circumstances or events which cause a pastor to deviate from the lectionary for the benefit of that congregation for a time. When these necessary periods of instruction are over, however, it is best for the pastor to return to the lectionary texts.

The Reading of the Texts

Each Sunday, three or four readings should be used. The lectionary has options each week for a psalm to be used in each service, but it is often neglected for the simple fear of making the service too long. One might also contend that the introit is a psalm reading, making another reading from a psalm unnecessary. While time constraints are an unfortunately necessary consideration, when possible, it is advisable that the psalm reading also be used.

In the Middle Ages, the Scripture readings were often chanted rather than spoken. This practice gradually disappeared after the Reformation and is no longer common in Protestant churches. Occasionally the gospel reading will be chanted by the minister, but the other two readings are spoken. The purpose of chanting in this context is to allow the people in the congregation to focus on the words of Scripture themselves, rather than the pastor's unique inflection and emphasis while reading. Though chanting the readings is not *necessary*, it is beneficial for the psalm, in particular, to be chanted antiphonally by the minister and the congregation since, as argued earlier, God gave the psalms to the church as songs, not poems.

In some congregations, lay readers read the Scripture lessons, while in others, the presiding minister reads all three texts. The practice of having separate lectors during a church service is an ancient one. If a church does have lay readers, they should perform their role in a proper manner. It is common for lay readers to forget that it is their turn to read on their assigned Sunday. They then run up to the lectern at the last minute not having prepared. They might have worn jeans and a T-shirt that Sunday, not having thought that they would perform any liturgical duty in front of the congregation, and then stumble through the words of the Scripture reading. In such a situation, it is better for the minister to read the Scripture. When lay readers are used, they must be prepared. The readings should be rehearsed prior to Sunday morning worship, and if possible, it is best for the lectors to also wear an alb. The alb covers the reader and puts the emphasis on the words of Scripture themselves, rather than on the person speaking. An alb also, again, serves as a picture of the white robes that all Christians will wear at Christ's second coming.

The Old Testament and epistle lessons are read at the lectern, and both of the readings lead to the gospel lesson, which is the most important of all three readings. This part of the service then culminates in the proclamation of God's Word through the sermon.

CHAPTER 7:
GOSPEL READING and SERMON

The previous aspects of the Service of the Word lead to the two most important parts of the non-Communion service: the reading of the Holy Gospel and the exposition of Scripture through preaching. These two actions constitute the climax of the first section of the Divine Service prior to the reception of Holy Communion.

The Gospel
Every Scripture reading in a church service is a monumental event, as the entirety of God's Word is breathed out by his Spirit (2 Tim. 3:16). God has attached himself to the Word in such a manner that every time these texts are read, the Holy Spirit is at work, both in convicting of sins by the law and in granting grace and mercy through the gospel. Though the gospels do not, in any sense, have a higher kind of inspiration than the rest of Scripture, the gospel readings have a higher place in the worship service than the epistle or Old Testament readings. The gospels are the most important aspect of God's Word because they are the story of the life, teachings, death, and resurrection of Jesus. The entirety of the Old Testament points toward the gospels, and the rest of the New Testament looks back to them. The gospels are central because *Christ* is central.

The centrality of the gospel is noted in a number of different manners through the liturgical actions surrounding its reading. The congregation remains seated during the Old Testament and epistle readings but stands for the gospel lesson. The act of standing is one of respect and reverence toward Christ who is described in the text. The gospel lesson will also usually be read by a pastor (or a liturgical deacon), even if lay readers are used for the other readings. In some congregations, the gospel lesson is chanted even if the other readings are spoken. It is also a common practice to have a gospel procession.

A gospel procession is a historic practice in both the Eastern and Western churches. It often includes the use of a separate "gospel book," which is a volume that contains only the four gospels. The practice of having a separate gospel book dates back to the fourth century, when the possession of an entire Bible was extremely rare. The gospel book can be used as part of the introductory procession with a deacon or other liturgical assistant carrying it forward behind the processional cross. These volumes are common in both Roman Catholic and Eastern Orthodox worship, where they have a prominent liturgical function. In the Eastern church, confession to a priest is made before a gospel book and crucifix. Though not extremely common, these books are sometimes used in Anglican and Lutheran churches.

If a procession occurs prior to the gospel reading, either a gospel book or a pulpit Bible will be used. If the gospel lesson is printed in the bulletin and read by the pastor, the bulletin page should not be used in a procession. For the gospel procession, a deacon or other liturgical assistant brings the Bible into the midst of the congregation as another assistant leads this procession with the processional cross. The assistants and the pastor stand in the midst of the congregation as the gospel is read by the pastor. The Bible or gospel book is held open by a liturgical assistant as the pastor reads. In many congregations, there is no gospel procession at all. In this case, sometimes the pastor will still walk into the midst of the congregation to read the gospel lesson, or he may read the gospel lesson either at the altar or from the lectern.

A song known as the Alleluia is connected to the reading of the Holy Gospel. After the congregation rises, with the announcement of the text of the gospel, the congregation repeatedly sings the word "Alleluia." This is a response to the grace that God gives through the reading of the gospel. The word *alleluia* literally means "praise Yah" (short for Yahweh) and is a common shout of praise used in Christian hymnody. At this point in the service, the Alleluia is specifically a praise to God for giving his inspired Word to the church. It is a recognition that the words read arise directly from God as they were inspired by the Holy Spirit. Not only were these words inspired in their original writing, but they continue to be accompanied by God's Holy Spirit as the hearers of God's Word are convicted by the law and set free through the gospel.

Hymn of the Day
Following the reading of the gospel, the congregation responds by saying (or singing), "Praise to you, O Christ," or something similar. The people then are seated, and the hymn of the day is sung in preparation for the sermon. As mentioned before, in a liturgical service, the music is not all sung at one particular time but is scattered throughout the service. This

continual return to singing emphasizes the dialogical nature of the service. Again, God gives, the congregation receives, and then God's people respond in praise. The hymn of the day follows the Scripture readings and thus continues the same theme of praise that is emphasized in the Alleluia. Praise is given both for the words that were just spoken and for the sermon that is about to be delivered from the pulpit.

The hymn of the day is the one hymn that is not connected to either the beginning or end of the worship service and is thus not tied to a processional. For this reason, the tone of this hymn might differ from the other two. The hymn of the day should reflect the time of the church year and particularly emphasize aspects of Scripture that are going to be expounded in the sermon. Singing this hymn is an act of praise and preparation wherein the congregants' hearts are prepared to receive God's Word as proclaimed by the minister.

In some congregations, a children's message is given. This can be done in the middle of the hymn of the day to give the pastor time during the latter half of the song to go to the pulpit and prepare for the message that he is about to give. Sometimes the children's message is done just before, or right after, the hymn of the day, but in these places, it is more likely to disrupt the order of the service. When a children's message is given, it should be a simple explanation of the theme of the sermon for that week. Too often, children's messages are simply moralistic in nature or are used simply to make the congregation get excited about how cute the children are. The children's message should be viewed as an extension of the sermon itself and must be taken as seriously as any instance wherein the Word of God is proclaimed in the worship service. The fact that it is for children does not change the minister's fundamental task of preaching law and gospel.

The Sermon

The proclamation of God's Word from the pulpit is the central action of the Service of the Word. In many older churches, the pulpit is raised in height. This custom has unfortunately been lost in most modern sanctuaries. The elevation of the pulpit emphasizes the centrality and importance of the preaching task. When the preacher moves to this location, a prophetic act is about to occur as the minister expounds upon the truths of God's Word to the congregation.

In the early church, preaching was central to Christian worship. This fact is attested in the book of Acts as well as several early manuscripts of Christian sermons given to various congregations. Some of the best preachers in Christian history were those of the first few centuries, such as "golden-mouthed" St. John Chrysostom and St. Ambrose of Milan. Though there were preaching movements throughout the entire history of the church, in the Middle Ages, the sacrifice of the Mass became more central to worship, and preaching was deemphasized. There were several reasons for this change, including low literacy rates and the frequency of church services. The Reformation was essentially a recovery of the centrality of God's Word in the church. The Renaissance, new systems and education, and the printing press allowed for a better education for clergy and access to Holy Scripture in its original languages. All of these factors contributed to the emphasis on preaching in the churches of the Reformation.

Though all branches of the Protestant Reformation emphasized the importance of preaching, some differences existed between various groups. Zwingli's reformation began with his preaching straight through the Gospel of Matthew. While doing this, he began to deconstruct the worship service, taking away its liturgical elements in an attempt to simplify worship. Luther, rather than abandoning the medieval Mass, retained essential elements of historic worship and viewed the sermon as an essential element of that liturgical service. The distinction, then, was that Zwingli had an almost exclusive emphasis on preaching in worship, whereas the Lutheran and Anglican churches viewed the sermon as one element (a central element) of the church's liturgical service.

The differences between the Lutheran, Anglican, and Reformed traditions surrounding preaching are apparent today if one visits churches from these movements. In a Reformed church, the sermon is usually longer, taking up a large portion, or perhaps the majority, of the worship service. Throughout the message, a particular text is exposited and explained in its theological content, historical context, and practical application. The message will often be based on a relatively small portion of Scripture, as the grammar of each verse is studied and explained to the congregation. This description was especially true in certain strands of Puritanism.

Within the Reformed church, there are two primary perspectives on preaching which continue to divide that tradition in the present day. First, there are some who follow a Puritanical approach, in which the pastor emphasizes practical application, especially as relates to killing sin and living unto holiness. Second, there is the redemptive-historical approach to preaching, wherein the pastor's role is to expound upon each text as part of the larger story of God's act of redemption in Christ.[48] Though these approaches differ, they both approach the task of preaching as primarily catechetical, and thus do not thoroughly differentiate preaching from Bible study.

More liturgical traditions tend to have shorter sermons. There are three primary reasons for this. First, the liturgical acts, alongside of the Scripture readings themselves, are part of the Service of the Word and thus fulfill a large part of what the Reformed would consider to be the task of preaching. Preaching is then one part of the broader service. Second, there is simply the practical concern of the length of the worship service. With a more elaborate liturgy, there simply is not the same amount of time left over to be devoted to the proclamation of God's Word from the pulpit. Third, there is a differentiation between preaching and Bible study. Both of these things are important for the people of God but serve different functions. In preaching, the pastor is to take the appointed text and apply it through law and gospel to the lives of his congregants. He does not explain every grammatical issue, textual variant, historical context, and so forth in each sermon. This is not to say that these considerations are absent from the pastor's preparation, but they are not central to the preaching task.

The time that the pastor has in the pulpit should be used wisely. Preaching is a sacred task, and it should not be treated lightly. The pulpit is not a place to tell entertaining stories or to deliver jokes to get laughs from the congregation. This is not to say that those things cannot supplement the main message of the pastor's sermon, but they are not *central.* Jokes, anecdotes, and the like are to be used only insofar as they help one to exposit the text under discussion. The sermon is not entertainment.

In the task of preaching, the minister is to proclaim God's judgment over sin as well as his grace toward sinners. This twofold proclamation has been the message of God's messengers since the foundation of the nation of Israel. A read through any of the prophetic books of the Old Testament reveals clear words of judgment and of liberation. This pattern continues throughout the epistles of the New Testament and the sermons described in Acts. Sin is revealed through

---

[48] On this debate, see Hyun, *Redemptive-Historical Hermeneutics*.

God's law (Rom. 3:20), and deliverance is revealed in the gospel (Rom. 1:16–17). This does not mean that every sermon has to follow a "first, law; then gospel" structure, but each element should be present and distinguished in a normal message delivered by the pastor.

Along with the proclamation of judgment and deliverance, the pastor is tasked with the duty to instruct his flock in Christian living (Tit. 2:1–13). The apostle Paul often follows the proclamation of forgiveness with admonitions unto holy living. These are often in the context of one's various stations in life; there are specific commands for a father, mother, child, master, servant, and so forth. The forgiveness of sins that is delivered in the gospel equips God's people for good works in this world. These duties are always to be proclaimed in light of the gospel so that one does not fall into a legalistic mindset. When preaching is simply a set of moral rules to follow, the Christian pulpit becomes no different from secular institutions that instruct in morality. The death and resurrection of Christ is always the central message of the church (1 Cor. 2:2).

The pulpit is also a place for catechesis. The pastor is called to teach and equip his congregation in Christian doctrine. If the lectionary readings are followed, then every major Christian doctrine will be taught each year as the text is exposited. Along with promoting orthodox doctrine, the pastor must also use his pulpit to rebuke false doctrine. Though the positive should have precedent over the negative, the rebuke of false teaching is a necessity, especially in a day when false teaching is so prominent. This area is one wherein some contemporary Lutheran preaching has fallen short. At one time, an average Lutheran sermon lasted around forty-five minutes. In such a long time frame, extensive catechesis was possible from the pulpit. In recent years, the sermon time has been significantly shortened, sometimes to as little as ten minutes. In such a small amount of time, it is difficult for one to do much other than speak law and then gospel concisely. It is not necessary to recover the practice of forty-five–minute sermons, but enough time should be given for preaching that the pastor can explain the text clearly and catechize. All this can be done well in around twenty minutes.

Every pastor will be different depending on his personality, and different congregational contexts will cause differences in the manner and mode of preaching. There is no single sermon structure that should be used in every message. One does not, for example, need to preach ten minutes of law and then ten minutes of gospel. Variety of structure is good and reflects the biblical pattern. Most importantly, the pastor should be proclaiming that which is taught in the particular text he has been given for that Sunday. A pastor should not use the pulpit to just preach about whatever he feels like talking about that day without regard for the text at hand. He fulfills his role as he speaks the Word of God as it has been revealed in Scripture.

CHAPTER 8:
CREEDS

The use of creeds and confessions is a debated topic in the contemporary church. It is common to hear people say, "No creed but Christ" or to claim that the Bible is the only confession of faith that is needed for the people of God. This ideology has been prominent especially in the American church since the Second Great Awakening (1790–1840). A movement known as the Restorationist Movement, or elsewhere called Campbellism, sought to establish a single unified church in the Unites States by getting rid of denominational barriers such as historic confessions of faith.[49] The intention was a new reformation in which all Christians would once again begin to work together. Though the intention for Christian unity is a noble one, the manner in which unity was sought only divided the church further as the congregations involved developed their own distinctive doctrines. The Restorationist Movement itself divided into a number of different groups that disagreed on various aspects of scriptural teaching.

The history of the Restorationist Movement demonstrates the necessity of having creeds and confessions in the church. While all claiming to believe strictly what the Bible teaches, these various congregations and church leaders continued to disagree about exactly *what* the Bible teaches. Whether they have written their confession of faith in a creed or not, a confession exists, even if only in their minds and preaching. The manner of thinking about the creeds that was prominent in the Campbell movement has continued to exist today. In non-denominational churches, creeds are not often spoken, though a church might include a small outline of basic beliefs on its congregational website. Such an outline is, in essence, a confession of faith. No church can simply say, "We believe in the Bible," without further qualification surrounding exactly what the Bible teaches. All Christians who are heirs of the Reformation desire to teach only what is revealed in God's Word, but they continue to disagree on exactly what is taught. Take an issue

---

[49] See Foster, *Encyclopedia*.

such as infant baptism, for example. In a church which claims to hold only to the Bible, the pastor might be convicted that the Bible teaches baptism by immersion for adults only. A member of that congregation might be convinced that Scripture teaches that infants ought to be baptized, and that baptism should be performed by sprinkling or pouring. Imagine that this member has a child and desires to get that infant baptized. What does a church do in such a situation? Should the pastor be forced to perform the act of infant baptism, which he believes to be unbiblical? Or should the parent act against his conscience and delay baptism? The fact is, every congregation has to face these kinds of questions. The way the church has historically chosen to address such issues is through creeds.

Creeds and *Sola Scriptura*
Those who reject the use of creeds often claim that the heavy emphasis on creeds is inconsistent with *sola scriptura*. One of the foundational principles of the Reformation, this Latin term professes that Scripture serves as the final authority in all faith and practice. No human tradition, creed, or council has been inspired by the Holy Spirit in the same manner as the words of Holy Scripture. If the creed is, in some sense, an authority in the church, some argue that it displaces the centrality of Scripture in guiding all beliefs of God's people.

A strong distinction must be made between the *source* of truth and the *expression* of that truth. The Bible is the only document given to the church directly by the inspiration of God (2 Tim. 3:16). It is thus the only document through which our doctrine is derived. The Bible has the final say in all issues of Christian doctrine. A creed serves a different function: it is the way in which the church expresses what it believes Scripture to teach. Think again about the example of the differing views on baptism. The confession of faith of one church that holds to believer's-only baptism might state, "We believe that baptism is properly given only to those who profess faith," while a church that holds to infant baptism might have something different in its confession, such as, "We believe that baptism should be administered to both believers and their children, including infants." Neither side in this discussion holds to its own position simply because its creed says so, but to the contrary, the creed says what it says because that is what those adherents believe Scripture to teach. Creeds and confessions give parameters for each church body and local congregation so that it is made clear what each church teaches.

Why Creeds Are Used in the Church

The use of Christian creeds was an extremely early practice in the church. Short confessions of faith appear in the New Testament itself and are apparent in some of the earliest Christian writings. These creeds were often written when specific heresies arose in the church so that false teachings might be guarded against. When a new issue arises in the church, it is often incumbent upon the church to make a statement surrounding that issue so that truth might be guarded against error. Connected with the use of creeds was the convening of church councils. When particular theological issues affected the church, a group of bishops, pastors, and other churchmen would gather together, discuss the issues in light of Scripture, and then decide what it was that the church believed. This practice dates back to the New Testament itself, where the Council of Jerusalem was convened to deal with issues surrounding the Mosaic Law (Acts 15).

When a church body adopts a creed, this action guards against the teaching of heresy. Pastors swear oaths to uphold the teachings of particular creeds in confessional traditions. This means that in a confessional church, every member can expect exactly what is to be taught and professed in the pulpit. If a church holds to the Nicene Creed, for example, one can expect that the pastor will not teach the congregation that Jesus is not divine. Creeds and confessions also allow a church body to keep its pastors accountable to a specific standard in their teaching. Christians with differing beliefs can also easily find churches that proclaim what they believe Scripture to teach. Someone who affirms infant baptism can simply look at the statements of faith of each local congregation and then have assurance as to what will be practiced in each church. A congregation is also assured that when calling a pastor, that pastor will hold to the same beliefs as that church.

Creeds in the Worship Service

In liturgical churches, creeds are not simply documents that remain in a book in the pastor's library, but they are to be accessible to the people. These creeds are used either before or after the preaching of the sermon. The entire congregation, not just the pastor, recites the creed. In proclaiming these words, the entire congregation professes its belief in these teachings of Holy Scripture in a short form. The creeds are written both in the first person singular ("I believe") and plural ("we believe").

The creeds are a confession both of the individual who is speaking those words and, simultaneously, of the entire congregation.

Traditionally, the Apostles' Creed, which is the shortest of the ecumenical creeds, is used at services in which Holy Communion is not celebrated. During a Communion service, the Nicene Creed is usually used. The third ecumenical creed, the Athanasian Creed, is recited only once a year, on the Feast of the Holy Trinity. Alongside of these, sections of the Small Catechism or other confessions of faith can be read during worship services.

The use of creeds within the context of worship is beneficial for the congregation. By reciting these words repeatedly in worship, the congregation is catechized in the basics of the Christian faith. While each member of the church might not think in depth about every article of the creed when speaking it on any given Sunday morning, these memorized words will impact the way in which congregants think about the Christian faith and understand Scripture. The creed equips the congregation to recognize heretical teachings. When someone from the Watchtower Society approaches one's door and informs him or her that Jesus is a creation of God the Father, phrases like "begotten, not made" and "of one substance with the Father" immediately come to mind, and the believer recognizes the incongruity between the statements being made and the teachings of Scripture. Since it is not likely that church members will memorize the entire Bible, these short statements of faith help the people commit to memory the basics of historic Christian theology.

The Scriptural Basis for Creeds

The use of creeds is ancient, extending back to the Old Testament. The Jews had a very simple confession of faith which became essential to their identity (and remains so today). This short confession, known as the *Shema*, is found in Deuteronomy 6:4: "Hear O Israel, the LORD our God, the LORD is one!" This short statement of faith is used to identify the God who is worshipped by the people of Israel. He is a single God, not a collection of gods. Unlike the surrounding pagan nations, this confession of faith identifies that the people of Israel are not polytheistic.

All later confessions of faith are essentially expansions of this one simple text. Like the *Shema*, all creeds serve the purposes of identifying the God of the worshipping community. Paul revises the *Shema* so that it identifies the deity of both the Father and the Son. Paul writes that "for us there is one God, the Father, of whom are all things, and we for Him; and one Lord Jesus Christ, through whom are all things, and through whom we live" (1 Cor. 8:6). Paul draws on the fact that the *Shema* identifies God by two distinct titles, "God" and "Lord." As a general rule, Paul speaks about the Son when using the term "Lord" and the Father when using the term "God."[50] This expansion of this early Jewish creed gives a further explanation of the identity of this one God of Israel, that he is two distinct persons: Father and Son.

This confession is still only a partial confession of God's identity, as Paul, in this short text, makes no mention of the Holy Spirit. The baptismal formula of Matthew 28 and other texts further clarify God's identity by acknowledging that God is Father, Son, and Holy Spirit. The church continued to draw upon these themes as it continued, of necessity, to clarify its expression of the faith.

Certain places in the New Testament contain what most scholars believe to be early Christian creeds. First Corinthians 15:3–8 contains a brief exposition of the gospel, in which Paul includes Christ's death, burial, and resurrection. This sequence is that which he "delivered to you" and "first received." This set of words served as an oral confession of the basic truths involved in the saving work of Christ. Paul also references what is either an early Christian hymn or an early confession surrounding Christ's humility in the *Carmen Christi* (hymn to Christ) in Philippians 2:6–11. These words, seemingly well known in the first-century church, serve as a means by which Paul encourages his readers unto humility in imitation of Christ. Other texts commonly thought to be early confessions of faith are in 1 Timothy 3:16 and Romans 10:9.

The use of confessions of faith has extensive scriptural warrant. The saints in Israel confessed the identity of their God in the *Shema* in opposition to the beliefs of the surrounding nations. Early Christians used that confession as a basis to further explain the identity of this God as Trinitarian. Additionally, a number of early creeds expanded upon aspects of Christ's saving work. The church continues to proclaim these creeds and confessions as a way of confessing the Christian faith to the unbelieving world.

The Ecumenical Creeds

There are three separate creeds which may be used as part of a liturgical

---

[50] See Fee, *Pauline Christology*.

service. These are known as the three ecumenical creeds. These statements of faith, known as the Apostles', Nicene, and Athanasian creeds, have been used by Christians for millennia and gradually became part of the regular worship of the church. Before we explore each creed, it is important to note that there are differences between the Eastern and Western churches in this area. The Apostles' Creed is used all across the Christian world, though there are differences in the understanding of the phrase "descended into hell" among a variety of traditions. The Nicene Creed, likewise, is used in churches of varying backgrounds in both the East and the West. East and West differ, however, in that the Eastern church does not recite the *filioque* clause ("and the Son") due to a theological disagreement.[51] This disagreement will be briefly addressed below. The Athanasian Creed, unlike the first two creeds, is not generally used in the Eastern churches in any form. Its absence is not due to any particular theological difference but is a product of that creed's Western origins. This is important to note, because in the fullest sense, it is only the Apostles' and Nicene Creeds which are truly ecumenical, and the Athanasian Creed functions in the same manner in only Western churches.

The Apostles' Creed
The most basic Christian confession of faith is the Apostles' Creed. Even in churches that do not have extensive confessions of faith or doctrinal statements, there is often a commitment to this basic statement of faith. In liturgical churches, the Apostles' Creed is often used in services without Holy Communion, while the Nicene Creed is used in Eucharistic services. The Apostles' Creed is also a very common catechetical resource. Luther's Small Catechism expounds upon each of the three articles of this creed, which frames a significant portion of catechesis.

This creed is, in some sense, the most ancient. Though it did not reach its current form until late in the fourth century,[52] there were a number of similar creeds used in the first centuries in the church; these eventually developed into the modern Apostles' Creed. The earliest form of this statement of faith appears in the writings of St. Irenaeus (AD 130–

---

[51] See Siecienski, *The Filioque*.
[52] There have been, however, some small changes since that time which took place in the early eighth century, such as the addition of the phrase "maker of heaven and earth."

202). In his treatise *Against Heresies*, he writes:

> [The church believes] in one God, the Father Almighty, Maker of heaven, and earth, and the sea, and all things that are in them; and in one Christ Jesus, the Son of God, who became incarnate for our salvation; and in the Holy Spirit, who proclaimed through the prophets the dispensations of God, and the advents, and the birth from a virgin, and the passion, and the resurrection from the dead, and the ascension into heaven in the flesh of the beloved Christ Jesus, our Lord, and His [future] manifestation from heaven in the glory of the Father "to gather all things in one," and to raise up anew all flesh of the whole human race, in order that to Christ Jesus, our Lord, and God, and Saviour, and King, according to the will of the invisible Father, "every knee should bow, of things in heaven, and things in earth, and things under the earth, and that every tongue should confess" to Him, and that He should execute just judgment towards all; that He may send "spiritual wickednesses," and the angels who transgressed and became apostates, together with the ungodly, and unrighteous, and wicked, and profane among men, into everlasting fire; but may, in the exercise of His grace, confer immortality on the righteous, and holy, and those who have kept His commandments, and have persevered in His love, some from the beginning, and others from their repentance, may surround them with everlasting glory.[53]

This creed of Irenaeus has some important similarities to the Apostles' Creed, and certain phrases are used verbatim in the statement that we know and use in the church today. Other places, however, clearly differ, as it would take a few centuries for the creed to become formalized.[54]

Irenaeus wrote his creed in a particular theological conflict; he wrote against an early Christian heretical sect called the Gnostics. There were a variety of Gnostic groups, and each had its own particular take

---

[53] Irenaeus, *Against Heresies*, Book I, X:1.
[54] Irenaeus is not the only church father to include something similar to the Apostles' Creed. Other similar statements can be found in Tertullian, Origen, Ambrose, and Augustine. This earlier form of the Apostles' Creed is often referred to as the "Old Roman Creed" to differentiate it from the more developed version which was finalized in the eighth century at the time of Charlemagne.

on the faith.[55] One of the unifying factors of these groups was that they downplayed the reality of the incarnation. Gnostics viewed the body not as a good gift of God, but as a prison from which the soul must escape. All that is material and physical was looked at with suspicion. The higher form of reality is non-physical. Thus, a physical incarnation and a physical resurrection were impossible. The creedal statements of men like Irenaeus helped guard the church against these Gnostic errors by emphasizing that the Christ was literally born, had a human body, and was raised in a human body. Like all creeds, the Apostles' Creed guards the church against false teaching.

Just as in the first centuries of the church, this creed continues to guard the church against errors. The Apostles' Creed confesses that Christ was "born of the Virgin Mary." In the nineteenth century, with the rise of Christian liberalism, a number of influential theologians began teaching that the virgin birth was simply a pious myth, not a historical reality. In my own life, I have encountered a number of pastors who, similarly, deny the historical reality of Christ's birth by a virgin. The Apostles' Creed guards God's people against such false teachings.

One of the most significant phrases in the entire creed is the words "under Pontius Pilate." With this phrase, the church confesses that the works of Christ that the creed enumerates happened at a particular point in history under the reign of this ruler. One cannot simply take the story of Christ's life as a nice myth or moral fable. The church presents it as actual history. Christ literally came to this earth, lived, died, and rose. There is no getting around a literal and physical resurrection from the dead in the Apostles' Creed. In this way, as with the virgin birth, the ancient words of the creed continue to guard and protect Christ's church from error.

The Apostles' Creed is divided into three articles. The first is about the work of creation in connection to God the Father. The second is about the work of redemption accomplished by Christ's work on earth. The third is about the Holy Spirit and his role in the application of redemption and the Christian church. The formulation is thus Trinitarian in nature, as the church confesses its belief in the three persons of the Triune God. The creed also covers the entire history of the world from creation through the consummation at Christ's return.

Everything in the Apostles' Creed is found in Scripture itself. If

---

[55] See Rudolph, *Gnosis*.

one were simply to combine the creedal statements within the New Testament, something very similar to the Apostles' Creed could be formulated.

The Nicene Creed

The more complex of the two creeds commonly used in Christian worship is the Nicene Creed. Similar in structure to the Apostles' Creed, the Nicene Creed speaks about the Trinitarian God and the works of creation, redemption, and sanctification. This creed is, however, a much longer statement of faith, especially as it expounds upon the nature of Christ as divine.

Like other creeds, the Nicene Creed was formulated in the midst of theological controversy, as a manner in which the church was able to define its beliefs surrounding the person of Christ. The particular controversy at issue was the Arian debate in the early fourth century. A bishop from Alexandria named Arius argued that "there was when the Son was not." He believed that the Son of God was not eternal or divine in essence. The Son was the first and greatest of all creation, but still a creation of God the Father rather than an eternal divine person. The debate over the deity of Christ continued for many centuries, and the position that Christ is fully divine was taken by a man named Athanasius, who became one of the most influential theologians in the history of the Christian church.

There were essentially three different parties involved in this debate. First, there were the Arians, who argued that the Son was *heteroousios* (of a different substance than the Father). Jesus is not divine. Others, known as semi-Arians, argued that the Son was *homoiousios* (of a similar substance to the Father). Though Christ is not divine, he is something *close* to divine. The third party were those following Athanasius, who argued that the Son is *homoousios* (of one substance with the Father). They argued that the Son has to be divine, or the entire essence of the Christian faith is lost. If Christ is not divine, salvation is impossible.

It seems somewhat strange that the entire church was split over what came down to essentially one letter. Was the Son *homoiousois* or *homoousois*? Though the terms themselves are almost identical, the difference between them is of utmost importance. If Christ is not fully divine, he should not be worshipped. He also is incapable of saving the human race. To be a perfect mediator, Christ must be both fully God and fully man. The Nicene Creed was formulated as the church's conclusion on these matters.

This debate over Christ's divinity was so heated that the then-emperor of the Roman Empire, Constantine, called a group of Christian bishops together to discuss the issues and formulate a definitive answer to the questions that were raised. This discussion occurred at the Council of Nicea in 325. This was the first of seven Ecumenical Councils, which were composed of representatives of the church from both the East and West to solve particular theological issues, usually relating to the person of Christ. Today, the Eastern Orthodox and Roman Catholic churches hold to the decisions of all seven councils, while Protestants generally differ from the decisions of the seventh.[56] All of these traditions, however, affirm the decisions of the Council of Nicea as definitive of Christian orthodoxy.

The Council of Nicea affirmed the belief of Athanasius that Christ is divine, and this affirmation was put together in the creed that is now known as the Nicene Creed. The most significant phrases in the creed in this regard are "begotten, not made" and "of one substance with the Father." The first phrase is a direct refutation of Arius's contention that the Son is a creation of the Father. Part of Arius's argument was from the biblical language of Christ's being "begotten" of the Father. Arius purported that the Son was begotten in the sense that a natural human son is begotten by his parents. By stating that Christ is begotten but not made, the creed recognizes that when Scripture speaks of the Son as begotten, it is not using the term in a natural human sense, but *analogously*, to speak of the eternal relationship between the Father and the Son. The second important phrase, "of one substance," is that debated term *homoousios*, which affirms that Christ is not only similar to God,

---

[56] The Seventh Ecumenical Council, also known as the Second Council of Nicea, met in 787 to discuss the use of images in Christian worship. The council itself decided not only that images of the person of Christ are to be used in worship, but that images of Christ and the saints are to be adored. The adoration of images is generally not a practice of Protestant churches. In Lutheran, and many Anglican, churches, images are used for pedagogical purposes, but not for adoration. Thus, it is common to see iconography in Lutheran sanctuaries. The Reformed tradition (and some Anglicans) has generally rejected the use of images in worship at all. Calvinistic theologians argue that images of Christ are a violation of the Second (what Lutherans call an appendix to the First) Commandment. Lutherans argue that the prohibition is of the worship of images, not of the use of images altogether.

but is himself a divine person.

The version of the Nicene Creed used in churches today is a modified form of this traditional statement of faith. It is sometimes called the Niceno-Constantinopolitan Creed, because it was, according to tradition, revised at the Council of Constantinople in 381.[57] The sections on Christ in the Niceno-Constantinopolitan form of the creed remain the same, but additional phrases are added to affirm faith in the Holy Ghost, who is similarly divine and worthy of worship, and to confess that baptism is for the remission of sins.[58] This third article adds to the Trinitarian structure of this creed, similar to the Apostles' Creed, and also refutes those who reject the divinity or personhood of the Holy Spirit.

Along with these additions at Constantinople, there was a further modification in the Western church that was not made in the East. At some point in the sixth century, some Western churches began to use the phrase "and the Son" to describe the procession of the Holy Spirit. This idea was rejected by the Eastern Orthodox churches and led to a split between the Eastern and Western churches in 1054 AD.[59] According to Orthodox theology, the Holy Spirit proceeds only from the Father, whereas Western theology, both Protestant and Roman Catholic, affirms that the Spirit proceeds from both the Father and the Son. This debate is quite complex, and a study such as this does not allow for an extensive explanation of the issues involved. It is important, however, to understand that these theological differences exist and account for the divergent wording of the Nicene Creed in these traditions.

The Nicene Creed has generally been connected to Holy Communion services, and it is spoken on any occasion when the Eucharist is celebrated. This statement of faith is essential for the church

---

[57] This is the traditional view, but it has been challenged by many today, who point out that there is no significant historical evidence from the documents of the Council of Constantinople itself that such a change occurred at the synod.

[58] Interestingly, Reformed churches that do not hold that baptism is literally "for the remission of sins" still continue to affirm the Nicene Creed. They believe that baptism is representative of the forgiveness of sins without actually granting such benefits directly. This interpretation of the phrase used in the creed is inconsistent with the church's beliefs in the fourth century, in which the affirmation of forgiveness through baptism was unanimous.

[59] This was not the only reason for such a split, however. Other factors included the language barrier between East and West, as well as debates surrounding the dating of Easter and the nature and role of the papacy.

today, because the same problems faced by Athanasius in the fourth century remain in the contemporary church. There are many sects who continue to deny the full divinity of Christ. The Jehovah's Witnesses teach, for example, that Christ is the archangel Michael, not a divine person. Similarly, they view the Holy Spirit as a force rather than a person. Some liberal traditions view Christ as a good human moral teacher rather than divine. The Nicene Creed continues to guard the church against these and other errors.

The Athanasian Creed
The third of the three ecumenical creeds is the Athanasian Creed. This is the longest and most theologically complex of these three statements of faith. Unlike the Nicene Creed, the Athanasian Creed was not written at an ecumenical council, nor was it written for the purpose of refuting one particular heresy. It is essentially an expansion of the teachings of the Nicene Creed and an extended exposition of the orthodox doctrine of the Holy Trinity.

The creed is named after St. Athanasius, who was the primary theologian behind the arguments that led to the Nicene Creed. One might get the mistaken impression that Athanasius wrote this creed, but that is not the case. It was written long after his death, probably at some point in the sixth century. The original text was written in Latin, and so it was used in the Western, Latin-speaking church rather than in the East. There is no record of the time or place of the writing of this statement of faith, but it has been used for many centuries in the Western church. The creed itself was likely put together specifically for use in public worship because the language of worship permeates this document.

It is a mistaken notion of many who have just begun to study church history that the Arians, criticized at the Council of Nicea, quickly disappeared after the First Ecumenical Council convened and rejected the Arians' teachings. Unfortunately, the Arian heresy took many centuries to gradually dissipate. Even today, it exists in some form. The Arians were a strong force for many centuries following the Council of Nicea, and they even convened their own councils, which condemned the decisions of Nicea. Thus, while the Athanasian Creed was probably not written with one particular council or controversy in mind, it was written at a time when many continued to reject the orthodox doctrine of the Trinity. The Athanasian Creed helps guard against the Arians and other groups who reject the deity of the Son and the personhood of the

Spirit.

Unlike the Apostles' Creed and the form of the Nicene Creed used in public worship, the Athanasian Creed includes not only a positive statement of doctrine but also a refutation of heresy. This statement of faith begins and ends with the assertion that all who are to be saved must hold to the beliefs outlined in this statement. Furthermore, all those who reject orthodox Trinitarian theology are doomed to everlasting perdition. These teachings are not just an exercise in the theoretical or philosophical issues that theologians like to discuss in an ivory tower; one's very salvation is at stake depending on who one confesses that God is.

In the Middle Ages, the Athanasian Creed was commonly confessed in public worship. Since that time, its use has gradually diminished. There is no particular theological reason for this decline. The creed is simply very long, and most congregations do not desire to repeat something so lengthy in each Sunday service. This does not mean, however, that the creed is never used today. It is read at least once a year, on the Feast of the Holy Trinity, when the church contemplates the mystery of the Triune God who has revealed himself in Scripture.

Other Creeds and Confessions

The three ecumenical creeds are the most essential confessions of faith for the entire Christian church. They outline the most fundamental aspects of the Christian faith and answer the question, "Who is God?" In these ways, the ecumenical creeds perform the same functions as the Old Testament *Shema* and the various New Testament creedal formulations. There are, however, alongside of these creeds, a number of more specific creeds used by various church traditions which are often used in the context of worship.

During the Reformation, various groups had to define their unique theological positions over against one another. The Council of Trent, in the Roman Church, defined a number of specific doctrines over against Luther and other reformers, such as the use of indulgences, the teaching of justification by both faith and works, and the necessity of the papacy. The Roman Church continues to convene councils and allows for the bishop of Rome to define dogma, which binds the hearts and minds of those in that communion. The Anglican, Lutheran, and Reformed traditions likewise created various statements of faith to define their own unique doctrines.

The Anglican church holds to the Thirty-nine Articles, which are included within the *Book of Common Prayer*, the common service book used in Anglican worship. These thirty-nine statements are distinctively Protestant and reject several tenants of Roman Catholic theology. The Reformed churches do not have one particular statement of faith but have developed several in differing locations and circumstances. The most commonly used today are the Three Forms of Unity (in the Dutch church) and the Westminster Confession (for those churches arising from the Puritan tradition). Sections of these documents are sometimes read during a worship service in a Calvinistic church. There is a tradition in Dutch churches of holding a Sunday evening service in which the pastor expounds upon the Heidelberg Catechism. In the Lutheran tradition, the 1580 *Book of Concord* is the norm of the theology of the church. This volume contains several documents, including the Augsburg Confession, the Apology of the Augsburg Confession, the Small Catechism, the Large Catechism, the Power and Primacy of the Pope, the Smalcald Articles, and the Formula of Concord. These documents inform the pastor's preaching, and portions are sometimes read in catechetical services.

In some congregations, new confessions of faith are used as a replacement for the historic ecumenical creeds. This practice is both unhelpful and unnecessary. The creeds that the church has traditionally used are not divinely inspired, but they have been tested by time and approved by churches throughout the world. A new confession of faith is not likely to express the faith as well as these older statements and disconnects that congregation from the church catholic, which uses universally accepted creeds.[60]

---

[60] One need look only at the recent Ligonier statement on Christology, in which a parachurch ministry has sought to formulate a new confession of faith on Christological issues. A number of bloggers quickly noted several theological issues in the statement. There simply is no reason to update or replace that which is already perfectly useful and orthodox. This incident at Ligonier also brings up the question of the authority of a parachurch organization to create a confession in the first place, apart from a church body's doing so.

CHAPTER 9:
PRAYER and the OFFERING

One of the most important aspects of Christian worship is prayer. Through Christ, the believer has the opportunity to approach God not as a wrathful judge, but as a father. God desires to hear the prayers of his saints, and the worship service gives us an opportunity to offer our prayers before our heavenly Father as members of his family.

Prayer in Scripture
Any student of the Bible knows that prayer is one of the central themes of divine revelation. From the beginning of the Old Testament through the end of the New, God invites people into his presence to commune with him. God created man in fellowship with him. God walked in the Garden of Eden with Adam as the two spoke with one another. Through sin, this relationship was broken, but through God's grace, the fellowship between God and man is restored. Prayer is a vital part of this relationship, as God invites us, through the forgiveness of sins, to speak with him.

Early Christian worship is defined in Scripture largely by prayer. In Acts 2, for example, Luke identifies early Christian worship with three acts: the teaching of doctrine, the breaking of bread (Holy Communion), and prayers. Four chapters later, the apostles define their ministry as consisting of two primary things: teaching and praying for the church (Acts 6:4). Deacons were appointed in the early church so that the apostles could spend more time in both prayer and teaching. Prayers thus are not simply a side note in worship, but an essential aspect of the public gathering of God's people, offered by both pastors and laity. The centrality of prayer is further demonstrated by the manner in which the New Testament epistles describe the importance of prayer as an act both of the church and of the apostles' ministry.

When writing to his student Timothy, Paul encourages the young man, saying, "I exhort first of all that supplications, prayers, intercessions, and giving of thanks be made for all men, for kings and all who are in authority, that we may lead a quiet and peaceable life in all godliness and reverence" (1 Tim. 2:1–2). According to Paul, the extent of the prayer offered by the church is universal. In verse four, Paul connects the universal nature of Christian prayer with the universal extent of Christ's atonement and God's love. Because God desires the salvation of all, the church should also pray for all. This message was particularly significant in the first century as Paul points out that even kings and those in authority are to be prayed for. The earliest church often viewed the authorities as enemies, as Nero and other Roman emperors persecuted those who confessed Jesus as Lord. In fact, Paul himself would be killed under the reign of Nero for his confession of faith. Yet even this fact did not change the reality that all people are in need of prayer.

In all of Paul's letters, there is a consistent emphasis on prayer for the churches to whom Paul is ministering. In Colossians, for example, Paul opens up his letter by mentioning that he continues to thank God for the faith and love demonstrated in the Colossian congregation (Col. 1:3–4). He tells the Colossians that he also prays for the church, and these prayers "do not cease" (Col. 1:9). The content of these prayers consists of supplications that these saints might grow in their knowledge of God and might perform good deeds for the sake of the world around them (Col. 1:10). These works are done in view of the redemption that Christ has won for the church and the eternal inheritance promised to those who trust in Christ (Col. 1:13–14). Paul's petitions serve as a model of prayer for those serving the church today, that we too might thank God for the faith worked in the saints, and that we would pray for God's continual sanctifying work within the church.

At the end of the Epistle of James, the apostle describes the nature of prayer within the church. In doing so, James notes that prayer should accompany all situations. He asks, "Is anyone among you suffering? Let him pray" (James 5:13). In difficult times, prayer should be upon the lips of both the one suffering and the fellowship to which that individual belongs. James mentions that in situations of sickness, the elders should pray and anoint with oil the one suffering (James 5:14). Prayer is also a means whereby one asks for the forgiveness of sins (James 5:15–16). The multifaceted nature of prayer is reflected in the corporate worship services.

Multiple books could be written examining just the New Testament passages concerning the nature of prayer. However, just this brief overview demonstrates a number of important points that inform the use of prayer in worship. First, as seen in Acts, prayer is an essential part of the church. Believers should continually be in prayer for one another, and it is one of the particular duties of those called to public ministry to spend much of their time in prayer. Second, prayer should be indiscriminate. We should pray for all people, both believer and unbeliever alike, including those who are enemies of the church. Third, we should pray for those in the church, both in thanking God for their faith and in asking that this faith might be strengthened. Fourth, prayer should accompany all times of life, especially times of suffering and sickness and when one falls into sin.

Prayer in the Divine Service
Prayer is not limited to one particular time in the worship service, as petitions are lifted up to God throughout the public worship of God's people. The *Kyrie*, collect, and certain hymns are prayers. Sometimes, an offertory prayer is said following the collection of the weekly offerings, and several prayers accompany the celebration of Holy Communion. There is one particular part of the service, however, when an extended amount of time is devoted to lifting up a number of specific petitions before God. This is often, in modern liturgical services, called the prayer of the church, though that title is not historic.

This time of prayer has not always been in the same place in the worship service. During the Reformation and in some earlier liturgies, the prayers generally occurred prior to the sermon, but in most services today, the prayers occur after. These prayers are usually in the form of petitions, asking God for help with a number of specific concerns both in the church and in the broader world. This time of prayer has historically taken two different modes. Sometimes (as in earlier American Lutheran liturgies) it is just an extended prayer of the pastor. The content remains the same each Sunday, with slight changes regarding the sick who are lifted up at this time. The other manner in which the prayers are said, which is probably more common today, is responsively. After each petition, there is a congregational response.

The use of responsive prayers in the service extends back to the Litany, which is a long prayer dating from the first centuries of the church. This lengthy prayer consisted of a number of petitions spoken by the pastor or deacon, with a response from the congregation following each petition. Forms of the Litany are found in both Eastern and Western churches. The Eastern form, known as the *Ektenia*, is a prominent aspect of public worship wherein both the petitions and the response are chanted. In the West, the lengthy Great Litany is used only on special occasions, and the Prayers of the Church or Bidding Prayer (the typical Anglican title) function in the same manner.

Each of these prayers contains a number of petitions dealing with a wide variety of subjects. While prayers can be spoken here which relate directly to the sermon, the day's theme should not be the only focus of the prayers, as these prayers function in a much broader capacity. Congregations often spend the majority of this time in prayer for those who are sick, both in the congregation and in the broader community. While asking God to help the sick is an important aspect of prayer, it also should not be emphasized to the exclusion of other concerns. In accord with Paul's admonition to Timothy, the prayers include petitions for those who are in authority in the nation as well as in the community. The Christian church throughout the world should be prayed for, especially in areas of persecution and martyrdom. The individual congregation's synod or communion should be prayed for, as should educational institutions and seminarians. Prayers for the military are also often included. Depending upon what service book is used, there will be a number of options of written prayers that can be spoken at this time. When there are special requests, the minister can add prayers.

The Offering

The prayers and the offering are not two separate acts in the service, but rather they are one unified aspect of worship. In both, the congregation lifts up thanks to God for his gracious provision and confesses its trust in him to respond. In prayer, believers confess their inability to provide for themselves and acknowledge God's divine goodness as he gives good gifts to his children. By offering up the money that they have, God's people confess that they give back to the one who has provided for them and trust that he will continue to provide. Both prayer and offering are also acts of thanksgiving in which the people offer themselves, their prayers, and their finances as a thank-offering to the God who has delivered them.

The giving of finances is an essential aspect of the life of the church. Without money, the church would simply not be able to function. It is necessary to pay for building expenses, the pastor's salary, missionary efforts, and many other worthwhile aspects of the life of the church. The offering of one's goods to God is not a new practice but extends back to the beginning of the Old Testament. Cain and Abel were called to give God offerings out of what they worked for (Gen. 4:2–5). As a worker of the ground, Cain offered plants, whereas Abel, as a shepherd, offered sheep. Offerings are further given to God by Noah, Abraham, and the other patriarchs. A tithe is specifically mentioned in the story of Abraham meeting the priest-king Melchizedek (Gen. 14:18–20). This principle of offering continues throughout redemptive history.

In the nation of Israel, God set up a specific form of offerings, both for himself and for the proper functioning of worship. After calling the Israelites out of slavery in Egypt, God gave his people an elaborate system of worship and sacrifice which required a large portion of their finances in order to function. Several of the instruments used in worship were made of gold and other precious stones. The tribe of Levi also needed to be provided for so that they could attend to their priestly duties. At this time, the Israelites had to offer a strict ten percent of all that they had to God. Along with this, they were required to purchase animals for sacrifice and a variety of other religious needs in the nation. There is not, however, an exact equation between this ten percent given to the government of Israel and that which is offered in church today. Israel was a theocracy, meaning that there was no strict division between church and state. This tithe functioned, therefore, not only as an offering for the religious needs of the people of Israel, but also as a tax. The people were also told to give to the poor in the nation so that those less fortunate might be provided for.

The tithe in the nation of Israel was strictly mandatory. One could no more avoid paying the tithe than one could avoid paying one's taxes today. This does not mean, of course, that the Jews were called to offer only the tithe. They could offer further goods to God, as in the practice of giving a freewill thank-offering. This offering of one's income to God was a sign of faith, of trust in God's provision for the nation. At times, it is even stated that the blessings given to the nation were dependent upon the tithe (Mal. 3:8–12).

Offering in the New Testament
There is some debate among Christians surrounding whether the tithe of the Old Testament is relevant to the church today. Some congregations require that a strict ten percent of the congregants' income must be given to the work of the church. To deny such an amount of money is disobedience to the commands of God. There are some significant problems with this position. First, the New Testament simply never says

that believers must give ten percent. Had God sincerely mandated that this be the case, he certainly would have included it in the text somewhere. Second, there is not an exact equation of the nation of Israel and the church. Just because something was mandated for the people of Israel, that does not mean that it is a necessary practice for God's people today. Third, the tithe in the Old Testament was both a tax and an offering to God. The separation between the church and the state today means that this rule cannot be strictly applied.

While the strict law surrounding ten percent of one's income might no longer retain validity, the principle of giving to the needs of the church does remain. There are several places in the New Testament where it is clear that God's people are called to offer money for the ministry of the church. In the book of Acts, the generosity of the early church is highlighted. It is mentioned that all goods were shared among believers such that the needs of everyone in the community might be met (Acts 2:44–45). It is also mentioned that the local congregations did not function autonomously but gave money to support other congregations (Acts 11:29–30).

Another important aspect of the finances of the church is the support of those who devote themselves to the pastoral ministry. God has always been concerned to provide for those who serve him in full-time ministry. In the Old Testament, the Levites were provided all of their necessities of life so that they could devote themselves completely to their service in the temple. Similarly, God has called those who make up the church's leadership today to devote themselves to prayer and teaching. This is why the church appointed deacons (Acts 6:1–4) who aided the apostles, thus giving the latter freedom to serve in their appointed roles without distraction. In several places, Paul mentions that the church should provide funds for those who minister (1 Tim. 5:17–18, 2 Cor. 11:8–9, Gal. 6:6, Phil. 4:15–18). In many circumstances, such as in a church plant or other small congregation, called pastors work a second job in order to support themselves and their families. Though often necessary, this situation is never desirable, and when possible, the pastor's needs should be met so that more time can be devoted to the ministry of the gospel.

Along with the expenses associated with the upkeep of a church building and the salary of pastors and other church workers, congregations should also devote money and other resources to the poor. God has always had a special concern for those who are needy. He set forth a number of laws in the Old Testament to ensure that the poor did not go without food; for example, he commanded those working the field to leave some of their crop for the needy (Lev. 23:22). One of the primary sins of the people of Israel which led to the Babylonian exile was their lack of concern for the poor (Amos 4:1). This principle of giving to the poor continues to apply to the church in the New Covenant. James mentions the necessary connection between a living faith and giving to those who are in need (James 2:15–16). Paul also instructs members of the Ephesian church to take care of the poor (Eph. 4:28). Through giving to the needy, the church expresses the same love that Christ has shown to the world in giving up his life.

The giving of finances to the church is an act of thanksgiving in response to God's grace. Like the rest of the service, this aspect of worship continues the pattern of God's giving and the congregation's consequently lifting up praises unto God. The offering is an act of praise and worship as an acknowledgement that these gifts (the financial resources) have been given by God. This offering need not be a strict ten percent, though that percentage remains a helpful guideline for giving. Ultimately, God informs us that our giving should be free and cheerful, not coerced through law (2 Cor. 9:7).

The Offering in the Worship Service

The offering is an opportunity for praise, and it is also an opportunity for the pastor to prepare for Holy Communion. The minister can spend this time both in prayer before the Service of the Sacrament and in getting the vessels for Holy Communion ready. The offering, then, serves as the bridge between the Service of the Word and the Service of the Sacrament.

A connection between the offering and Holy Communion is ancient. The church father Hippolytus (170–235) mentions that offerings were given by the congregation as part of the Communion service itself. Following the preface, the congregation would bring forward several forms of offering such as oil, cheese, and olives. Though this practice no longer remains, the connection between thank-offerings and Holy Communion does. The very name *Eucharist* means "thanksgiving." Jesus, before giving his body and blood to his disciples at the Last Supper, gave thanks. Today, the church continues to give thanks, not only in the Communion prayer, but through the offering prior to the Eucharistic celebration. This giving of thanks is done in view of the previous gifts provided by God and in anticipation of the gift of Christ's body and blood in the Supper.

Following the collection of the offering, a hymn is sung by the congregation, demonstrating the continual manner in which thanks are given to God for his provision. There are several hymns or psalms that have been used here throughout the centuries. The offerings are then brought forward to the altar, where the minister blesses them. Though an offertory prayer is no longer as common as it once was, it is still a good practice: the congregation asks for God's blessings upon the gifts that they have given, that these gifts might be used for the building up of God's kingdom.

With the offering, the Service of the Word comes to an end. In a service without Holy Communion, the Lord's Prayer follows the offering along with a benediction and closing hymn. When the Lord's Supper is celebrated, the focus then shifts to the gift of Christ's true body and blood that are given on the altar.

CHAPTER 10:
HOLY COMMUNION

The service of Holy Communion is at the heart of Christian faith and life. In this sacrament, two essential realities occur for the benefit of God's people. First, God gives us his Son's true body and blood, through which we receive the forgiveness of sins. Second, the people of God's church are joined with one another as we share a mysterious and intimate bond as fellow members of Christ's body. This sacrament, together with the proclamation of God's Word, lies at the core of Christian worship.

The Place of Holy Communion in Worship
There are a variety of traditions surrounding the Eucharist and exactly what its place is for the people of God. A church's particular theology of Holy Communion greatly affects its order of service and structure of worship. The disagreements between the Lutheran, Zwinglian, and Roman Catholic traditions lead to distinctively different practices in each theological tradition.

In the Reformed church, Holy Communion has not remained as central to the worship of God's people as it has in more formal liturgical traditions. This is not to say that Communion is unimportant for the Reformed, or that the Sacrament takes on a purely symbolic character. Though Zwingli limited the Sacrament almost exclusively to a memorial feast, Calvin argued that the believer truly partakes of Christ by faith.[61] Yet Calvin still rejected Luther's realism in the Sacrament. Christ's presence was viewed as a spiritual one, and the body and blood of Christ were not viewed as literally present on the altar. Instead, the human nature of Christ remains in heaven. In Geneva, though Calvin desired to celebrate frequent Communion, the Sacrament was received only four times a year. The celebration of the Lord's Supper remains infrequent in many Reformed churches.

Though an important aspect of worship, the Eucharist is subordinated to the Word in Calvinistic services. Reformed churches rid

---

[61] See Mathison, *Given for You*.

themselves of the use of an altar, and the center of the sanctuary is not the communion table, but the pulpit. The sermon tends to be lengthier than in more liturgical services, and there is not an extensive amount of liturgical action surrounding the sacrament of Holy Communion.

In contrast to the Reformed tradition, the Roman Catholic Church views the celebration of the Eucharist as *the* central part of Christian worship. Through this action, according to the Roman tradition, Christ's sacrifice is re-presented on the altar by the priest. This Mass is an unbloody sacrifice offered on behalf of both the living and the dead. Often, Masses are performed without anyone other than the priest present (these are often referred to as "private Masses") and grant the benefits of the atonement even apart from personal reception of the elements. This unique view of the Sacrament of the Altar causes the Roman Church to deemphasize the importance of the Word of God and its proclamation in the pulpit. In the Roman Church, homilies are short and generally serve to lead one to the more important aspect of worship in the Eucharistic sacrifice.

The Lutheran tradition often uses the phrase "Word and Sacrament" to describe its ministry. Both elements of worship are absolutely essential. One should not be privileged over the other. At certain times in Lutheran history, aspects of other traditions have changed the manner in which the worship service was viewed. In Lutheran Pietism, the Lord's Supper was not explained as a central means of grace, since Bible study and preaching (including lay preaching) were emphasized. Infrequent Communion, as in the Reformed tradition, eventually became the norm in many Lutheran churches.

In the late nineteenth century, a liturgical renewal began under the influence of Wilhelm Loehe. This liturgical renewal continued in the twentieth century as theologians began discussing the importance of historic worship and frequent Communion. Missouri Synod theologian Arthur Carl Piepkorn, among others, argued for the distinctiveness of the Lutheran Reformation over against the majority of Protestantism. Since that time, the practice of weekly Communion has been restored in many parishes, and the Sacrament has regained its central place in Christian worship.[62]

While the theology and practice surrounding the Eucharist have been emphasized since the mid-twentieth century in Lutheranism, the

---

[62] See Wieting, *Weekly Communion*.

length of sermons has continually decreased. Because many Lutherans today emphasize the distinctiveness of Lutheranism in contradistinction to broader Evangelicalism, there might be a tendency to overemphasize the Sacrament and to deemphasize the importance of preaching. The Lutheran church, at its best, retains the importance of both Word *and* Sacrament, without privileging one to the neglect of the other.

The Preface
Following the offerings, the focus of worship shifts. No longer are God's people anticipating and rejoicing in the proclamation of God's Word from the pulpit, but they begin to prepare themselves for the distribution of Christ's body and blood under the forms of bread and wine. The remainder of the Divine Service centers on the altar, where these gifts are distributed.

There are three different aspects of the Service of the Sacrament which occur each time the Lord's Supper is celebrated. First is the preface. This is the introductory aspect of the Communion service, when the people of God are invited into God's presence to partake of this mystery. This portion of the service begins with the salutation and concludes with the *Sanctus*, as the congregation sings, "Holy, holy, holy." Second, and most central, are the consecration and administration of the Sacrament. This part consists of the Eucharistic prayers, the words of institution, and the giving of the Supper. This portion of the service ends with the blessing given by the pastor to those communing. The final element of the Service of the Sacrament is the post-Communion service, which begins with the *Nunc Dimittis* (or alternatively, "Thank the Lord") and ends with the close of the service.

In the early church, not everyone was allowed to remain in the Service of the Sacrament. Following the Service of the Word, catechumens and other visitors who had not yet received Holy Baptism were dismissed from the place of worship. It was understood that the Sacrament was limited to those who were already members of the body of Christ. Those learning about the Christian faith anticipated the day in which they would remain for the celebration of Holy Communion and partake of this mystery which God grants to his people. Though this dismissal is no longer practiced in a strict manner, the Lord's Supper continues to be restricted to those who have been baptized and are members of the body of Christ.

As the preface opens, the pastor greets those who are gathered to celebrate the Supper. He begins with the words, "The Lord be with you." This type of greeting is common in Scripture; for example, St. Paul writes to the Corinthians, "The grace of our Lord Jesus Christ be with you" (1 Cor. 16:23). Through these words, the pastor invites the people of God into worship with him. The congregation then responds by saying, "And also with you," or the older form, "And with thy spirit." This greeting again emphasizes the nature of dialogue in the worship service between the congregation, the pastor, and God. All parties are active when gathered together for corporate worship.

Following the greeting, the pastor speaks the *Sursum Corda*, which consists of the words, "Lift up your hearts," with the congregation's response, "We lift them unto the Lord." With these words, the pastor calls the people of God to take their eyes off of all earthly worries and troubles and to focus their hearts on heaven. During the celebration of the Eucharist, heaven comes down to earth as God enters into the presence of his people. The affections of God's people are lifted up to him, and God subsequently enters into the presence of the saints. After this encouragement to the people, the pastor then invites the congregation to give thanks to the Triune God, and the people respond with the words, "It is right to give him thanks and praise." These thanks and praise are given to God in view of the gift which God is about to bestow upon his people. The Lord's Supper brings communion with God, the forgiveness of sins, and the strengthening of faith.

The preface is an ancient aspect of Christian liturgy. St. Hippolytus mentions that in the early third century, Christians were using a preface in worship with the following structure:

> The bishop says: The Lord be with you.
> And all reply: And with your spirit.
> The bishop says: Lift up your hearts.
> The people respond: We have them with the Lord.
> The bishop says: Let us give thanks to the Lord.
> The people respond: It is proper and just.[63]

It is remarkable that this basic structure has remained the same for as long as we have record of the nature of the Eucharistic service. This fact is a great reminder to the people of God that in worship, the church

---

[63] Hippolytus, *Apostolic Tradition*.

across the ages joins together in the act of praising the Triune God and receiving Christ's body and blood.

During the opening part of the preface, the pastor faces the people rather than the altar, since he is speaking directly to the people. Generally, his hands will be held out as a gesture of greeting, and then up in the *orans* position as he asks the congregants to lift up their hearts to God. Following the request to give thanks unto God, the pastor then moves from his prophetic to priestly mode as he again leads the people in prayer.

The Proper Preface

While entering into the position and attitude of prayer, the pastor chants or speaks the proper preface. This section of the liturgy changes at different points during the church year in accord with the current season or day of the calendar. Different prefaces are used for Advent, Lent, Easter, Christmas, Pentecost, and Holy Trinity. The words of each preface, though similar in structure, differ in the aspect of redemptive history that is recited.

The preface follows a particular structure. In the East, the same preface is used for each service, and it begins with the act of creation, followed by a lengthy exposition of salvation history. In the West, the preface is shorter and changes. The preface is essentially a song of praise. It begins with the pastor's extolling the necessity and benefit of praising God at all times for the gifts he bestows upon creation. Such praise is beneficial "at all times and in all places." There is no circumstance in which God should not be praised.

This preface includes language about both the church militant and the church triumphant. It is with "angels and archangels, and all of the company of heaven" that the congregation praises the Triune God. The phrase quoted above serves as a reminder, again, that worship includes the union of heaven and earth as the church gathers together. Christians do not worship alone, but with all of the heavenly host. Liturgical worship involves the congregation's becoming involved in the worship that occurs in heaven before the throne of God. Worship breaks down the barrier between heaven and earth. This language purposefully brings to mind the worship scenes throughout the book of Revelation.

This portion of the liturgy is usually chanted, though it is sometimes spoken. The prayer itself has roots in a variety of Jewish prayers surrounding the celebration of Passover. References to thanksgiving prayers around this feast date back at least to *Hillel* in the first century. These Jewish prayers were often chanted rather than spoken. Thus, the church likely picked up the practice of chanting prayers from their Jewish antecedents. The specific tones that are used in the Western church for the proper preface date back to the beginning of the eleventh century without much variation. They are thus almost universally used in the Western church.

The Sanctus
At the end of the preface, the minister announces that the congregation will sing together the song of the saints and angels in heaven with the chorus "Holy, holy, holy." These words serve as a reminder to the congregation that the holy Triune God himself is present in worship and that they are welcomed into that holy presence through the grace of Christ.

This hymn, the *Sanctus*, is first mentioned in the book of Isaiah. The prophet was caught up into the presence of God, into God's heavenly throne room. Isaiah describes two seraphim before God's throne who speak these words:

> Holy, holy, holy is the LORD of hosts;
> The whole earth is full of His glory! (Is. 6:3)

That the word *holy* is repeated three times in this hymn is significant for two reasons. First, the repetition of a word emphasizes its importance. For example, when Jesus is about to make a very important point during his ministry, he uses the formula, "Truly, truly, I say to you."[64] God's holiness is his only attribute that is repeatedly praised three times in this manner. Second, the threefold repetition of this word demonstrates the Trinitarian nature of worship. The angels in Isaiah's vision worship the Father, Son, and Holy Spirit as holy. Similarly, the worship of the church is Trinitarian, as all three persons of the Godhead are honored and worshipped.

In this way, the worship of the church militant mirrors the worship of the church triumphant. The book of Revelation, like Isaiah, includes the *Sanctus* as an essential part of heavenly praise. The four living

---

[64] Those who use the KJV will be more familiar with the older rendition, "Verily, verily."

creatures who sit before the throne of Christ, like the seraphim, sing,

> Holy, holy, holy,
> Lord God Almighty,
> Who was and is and is to come! (Rev. 4:8)

Though the words following it differ, the trifold repetition of God's holiness remains in both texts. This Trinitarian praise echoes throughout the church militant, as well as from the mouths of the seraphim, the living creatures, and the saints in heaven.

Conclusion

All of the elements of worship discussed in this chapter prepare the people of God for the central part of this service, as they receive Christ's true body and blood. This reception of the Lord's Supper has many benefits, including the union of heaven and earth before the throne of Christ; the forgiveness of sins, for which the church offers praise and thanksgiving; and the unity of God's people on earth.

CHAPTER 11:
EUCHARISTIC PRAYERS

While there is a broad agreement among Lutheran theologians and pastors about the nature of the liturgical worship service, there is quite a bit of debate surrounding the usefulness and appropriateness of Eucharistic prayers. These prayers, which accompany the service of Holy Communion following the *Sanctus*, are not present in all orders of service,[65] but they have become more common within the last century in Lutheran congregations.

The Reason for Debate
The appropriateness of prayers at any point in the service might seem like a rather strange point to debate, as prayers occur throughout the worship service. There is, however, a particular theological concern which drives the debate in this area. Before some of the contemporary debates can be addressed, some background about these prayers in the Roman tradition must be briefly explained.

In the gospel narratives, the Lord's Supper is portrayed as a gift of God, through which God serves his people. Prior to his being betrayed by Judas and his consequent arrest and crucifixion, Christ offers the Passover meal to his disciples. This meal is identified with Christ's body and blood, which are given for the forgiveness of sins. Over the centuries, the nature of the Lord's Supper as a pure gift from Christ to the people of God began to become distorted, and the direction of Holy Communion began to change. Rather than being seen as a divine gift, the Supper was viewed as a human offering given to appease the wrath of God.

The Roman Catholic Church, both in the Middle Ages and today, emphasizes the man-to-God nature of Holy Communion, especially in its prayers. In the Roman Canon, some of the following prayers are said as part of the Eucharistic service:

> Through [Christ] we ask you to accept and bless + these gifts we

---

[65] See *Lutheran Service Book*, Divine Service: Setting Three.

offer you in sacrifice.

We offer you this sacrifice of praise for ourselves and those who are dear to us. We pray to you, our living and true God, for our well-being and redemption.

Bless and approve our offering; make it acceptable to you, an offering in spirit and in truth. Let it become for us the body and blood of Jesus Christ, your only Son, our Lord.

Almighty God, we pray that your angel may take this sacrifice to your altar in heaven.[66]

All of these prayers speak about Holy Communion as a sacrifice that the church offers to God rather than something that God offers to us, which we simply receive.

The purpose of the Lord's Supper is one of the most important areas in which the Lutheran and Roman traditions differ. While we share a common sacramental heritage and emphasis, and both affirm the true presence and reception of Christ's body and blood in the Sacrament, there is an essential theological difference regarding the direction that the Eucharist takes. For the Roman Church, the direction of Communion is from the church to God, as this sacrifice is offered to the Father in order to appease his wrath. For the Lutheran church, Holy Communion is a divine gift that needs simply to be received.

When Martin Luther made his liturgical reforms, he took the nature of Holy Communion into great consideration. Luther argued that there is an essential difference between a *sacrament* and a *sacrifice*. A sacrament, according to the reformer, is a gift which God gives that has the promise of forgiveness attached to it. A sacrifice, on the other hand, is something that a human creature offers to God for forgiveness. Luther was concerned that the Lord's Supper be treated as a sacrament rather than a sacrifice, as it unfortunately had been viewed as in his time. Because of this misunderstanding, Luther excised the entire canon from the Mass. In his 1526 *Deutsche Messe* (German Mass), Luther eliminated all prayers during the Service of the Sacrament other than the Lord's Prayer. For some Lutherans, this shorter form of Communion is seen as

---

[66] Eucharistic Prayer I, *Catholic Liturgical Library*.

standard for the Lutheran church.

There were two important theological and practical reasons why Luther eliminated all Eucharistic prayers in the worship service. The first is that which has been explained above. The prayers shift the direction of the Communion service. Rather than highlighting God's giving to his people, the prayers emphasize the work of the congregation toward God. This was especially true at Luther's time because of the precise *kind* of prayers that the church prayed then. The second reason is that Luther wanted to ensure that the emphasis in the Service of the Sacrament was on the words of Christ. Unfortunately, with all of the prayers and pageantry surrounding the Sacrament, the words of institution became less central. For Luther, it is the Word of God which makes the Sacrament efficacious. These words of institution are the most important part of the Holy Communion service and should be treated as such. This belief of Luther's resulted in his insistence that the words be chanted out loud and his defense of the bare *Verba* (the words of institution alone).

While the use of only the words of institution is an acceptable and historic Lutheran practice, there are several positive reasons to include Eucharistic prayers in worship. First and foremost, however, it must be emphasized that the nature of these prayers must always reflect the downward nature of the Sacrament. The Lord's Supper is most certainly a sacrament rather than a sacrifice, to use Luther's terminology. Any prayer which confuses the direction of the Supper in this manner is not to be used in public worship. It is better to have no prayers than ones which emphasize a confusing and unbiblical theology.

There are three reasons why Eucharistic prayers can be a beneficial addition to the worship service. First, there is simply no time in which the Christian should not offer himself up to God in prayer. The Apostle Paul tells us that our prayers should be made "without ceasing" (1 Thess. 5:17). Similarly, in the proper preface, the pastor says that it is right "in all times and in all places" to give thanks to God. Holy Communion is not an exception to this rule, as if God desires the prayers of his people at all times other than during the reception of the Lord's Supper. To the contrary, what better time is there for God's people to offer their praise and thanks to God than prior to receiving one of God's greatest gifts? Second, this practice is historic. The earliest records of Communion services describe a variety of Eucharistic prayers. This practice was likely taken from Judaism and may extend back to the apostles themselves. Generally, the Lutheran church has sought to retain historic Christian worship in all areas excepting those in which false theology is taught. Finally, the giving of thanks is part of the Last Supper narrative itself. Jesus gives the disciples his body and blood right after "giving thanks," which is surely a reference to Jewish paschal prayers. If Christ prays just prior to speaking the words of institution, why would it be wrong for us to do the same?

There is, ultimately, no strict scriptural command concerning Communion prayers. We therefore cannot mandate that they should or should not be used. Both practices exist in Lutheran congregations, and Eucharistic prayers should be allowed unless a congregation starts using prayers that emphasize a wrong view of the Sacrament. What is most important is that the words of institution be spoken each time the Eucharist is celebrated. These are the words that Jesus commanded, and it is through these words that God makes the Sacrament efficacious for the forgiveness of sins.

The Lord's Prayer

Even in those traditions that reject most Eucharistic prayers, the Lord's Prayer is still used at some point during the Service of the Sacrament. The connection between the Lord's Prayer and Holy Communion is ancient. It appears at this portion of the service in the most ancient liturgies available. It even retains this position in certain congregations which do not heavily follow the historic liturgy.

The Lord's Prayer is the only prayer directly given by Jesus in the New Testament. It is given in two separate accounts: Matthew 6:9–13 and Luke 11:2–4. Jesus speaks these words in the Sermon on the Mount in response to false forms of piety practiced by many of the Pharisees. These words are not simply a structure for prayer, but they also give us specific words which should be used when Christ's disciples speak to their heavenly Father. Memorized prayers were often used in first-century Judaism, and the disciples would have understood the words of Jesus in such a context.

Christians have adopted the Lord's Prayer in worship from the beginning of the church. An early Christian document called the *Didache* (the "teaching") mentions that believers should pray these words at least three times daily (*Didache* 8:2–3). The Lord's Prayer served for both private and public prayer. The churches of the Reformation continued to emphasize this prayer, and Martin Luther included it as one of the chief parts of his Small Catechism.

Aspects of the Eucharistic Prayer

Historically, there have been three primary aspects to Eucharistic prayers. These are the thanksgiving, the anamnesis, and the epiclesis. Roman, Anglican, Eastern, and even many Reformed liturgies use each of these elements in one way or another. It is the Lutheran tradition alone which has largely removed them from use in the worship service. Many contemporary Lutheran hymnals have (fortunately) reintroduced each of these aspects into the Service of Holy Communion.

One contemporary example of the use of Eucharistic prayers in Lutheran worship is from Divine Service: Setting One in the Missouri Synod's hymnal *Lutheran Service Book*. This book contains five separate settings for use in worship, including one based on the Common Service and another on Luther's *Deutsche Messe*, which both contain the bare *Verba*. In contrast to this, the first service setting presents an opportunity for congregations to include a fuller Eucharistic service, which includes two of the three historic aspects of Holy Communion prayers in connection with the words of institution.

Following the singing of the *Sanctus*, the service continues with the post-*Sanctus* prayer, which is a prayer of thanksgiving. This prayer begins with an address to God the Father, thanking him for both creation and redemption. Special attention is then given to Christ's acts of redemption accomplished on behalf of the human race as outlined in the creed. The very benefits of Christ's work are about to be received by the faithful through eating and drinking the body and blood of Christ. The prayer then requests that God would help his saints to receive these gifts in faith and ends with a Trinitarian invocation. The idea of thanksgiving is essential as part of the Holy Communion service. The term "Eucharist" literally means "thanksgiving"; this is a time of giving thanks. Though the body and blood of Christ are not sacrificed during the celebration of Holy Communion, Christians are called to offer *themselves* as thank-offerings unto God for the gifts that he bestows upon the congregation (Rom. 12:1).

The second aspect of Eucharistic prayers, which is not common in Lutheran worship, is the epiclesis. The epiclesis is an invocation of the Holy Spirit to sanctify the elements of Communion. This is usually included at the end of the prayer of thanksgiving, wherein God is entreated in order that the Spirit might be sent to sanctify the elements as well as those who are receiving these elements in faith. In the Eastern

Church, the epiclesis has a much more central role than it does in Western theology. While the West speaks about the words of institution as the time in which God sanctifies the elements, in the East, that time is identified with the invocation of the Spirit. The consecratory epiclesis is the asking of the Holy Spirit to descend upon the elements of Holy Communion and to sanctify them through making them to become the body and blood of Christ. This type of epiclesis is not generally used in Lutheran worship, because Scripture never speaks of such an invocation as causing the elements to become Christ's body and blood. Instead, Jesus simply gives the words of institution. Those words are, themselves, efficacious to effect the change necessary for the reception of Christ's true body and blood.

Although the invocation of the Holy Spirit upon the elements themselves is not to be preferred in Lutheran worship, there is a second type of epiclesis. This is sometimes referred to as the "epiclesis of communion" in which God's people ask the Holy Spirit to descend upon the worshipping community in order to strengthen the faith and unity of believers through the Sacrament. Such a practice is historic and can be used faithfully in a Lutheran service, though still, it remains uncommon. The fourth setting of the Divine Service in the *Lutheran Service Book*[67] contains a short epiclesis with the words, "Grant us your Holy Spirit that we may faithfully eat and drink of the fruits of His cross and receive the blessings of forgiveness, life, and salvation that come to us in His body and blood."[68] This petition, or something similar, can be used at the end of the prayer of thanksgiving.

The final aspect of the Eucharistic prayers is the anamnesis, or "remembrance." This portion of the prayer is a recitation of the acts of redemption accomplished by Christ for the world's salvation. It often includes five specific points of Christ's work: his death, his rest in the tomb, his resurrection, his ascension, and his return for final judgment. In speaking of these events, the church obeys Christ's command to celebrate the Lord's Supper as a remembrance. In this feast, all of the benefits of Christ's work are given, and the church confesses these truths prior to receiving those benefits. Following this act of remembrance, the

---

[67] I cite this example because this is the hymnal with which I am most familiar. Though my congregation is in the American Association of Lutheran Churches, we use Setting One in the *Lutheran Service Book* (published by the Lutheran Church—Missouri Synod) for all Holy Communion services.

[68] *Lutheran Service Book*, 209.

pastor speaks the words of institution as the Sacrament is consecrated.

CHAPTER 12:
The WORDS of INSTITUTION

As important as the prayers may be, the words of institution remain the most central aspect of the service of Holy Communion. These words were given by Christ to the church as the words which should be spoken when his people celebrate the Sacrament. Whatever else is present in the celebration of the Lord's Supper, these words are an absolute necessity.

Interpreting the Words of Institution
The words of institution are given in four separate places in Holy Scripture. They are cited by all three Synoptic Gospels, and Paul mentions them as the tradition passed on to the Corinthians in their order of service (1 Cor. 11:23–25). Though there are some slight differences in the wording of each account, the basic formula remains the same: Christ identifies the Sacrament with his body and blood given for the forgiveness of sins. Since four accounts of the Last Supper in the New Testament contain these statements, they are portrayed as central to its celebration.

These words have been heavily debated throughout the history of the church. Especially during the time of the Reformation, the exact nature of Christ's presence in the Lord's Supper became a central point of concern. The Roman tradition, at least since the Fourth Lateran Council in 1215, has argued for a doctrine of transubstantiation, wherein the elements, when consecrated, become the body and blood of Christ. When Jesus says, "This is my body," he is literally identifying his body with the element in his hand. When separating from the Roman Church, Ulrich Zwingli argued that this medieval notion of sacramental realism was mistaken. Instead, the Swiss reformer purported that the elements simply *represent* Christ's body and blood. The meaning of the words of institution, then, is not that believers receive Christ's actual body and blood, but that the body and blood are simply signified in the memorial meal.[69]

---

[69] On these debates see Sasse, *This Is My Body*.

The Lutheran Reformation, though rejecting transubstantiation, heartily affirms the truthfulness and literal meaning of Christ's words. In the Supper, one receives Christ's actual body and blood. This is not simply a memorial. The words of institution, then, have a very prominent position within the Lutheran liturgy. This prominence is part of the reason for the excision of the Eucharistic prayers in early Lutheranism, and it is also the reason why Luther preferred that the words themselves be chanted rather than spoken. In most modern services, these words are not sung; in fact, in most service settings, no chant tones are given for the words of institution. Though, again, there is no divine command whether to speak or chant these words, chanting brings attention to the solemnity and majesty of what occurs during the Eucharistic service, as the true Christ is present upon the altar.

The Blessing and Elevation

While speaking the words of institution, the pastor makes the sign of the cross over the elements which are going to be consumed during the service of Holy Communion. In this way, he blesses the elements and sets apart these particular instruments as the vehicles by which the congregation receives Christ. Notably, Paul mentions that the cup of which one partakes in the Sacrament is the "cup that we bless" (1 Cor. 10:16). This blessing mirrors the one given over the offering, wherein the financial gifts of God's people are set apart for holy use. Similarly, the service closes with a Trinitarian blessing during the benediction.

Along with this blessing in the Eucharist, the pastor may lift up the host. This practice is often called the elevation of the host. The same may also be done with the chalice. The practice of lifting up the elements during the celebration of Holy Communion is not an ancient one, but it developed in the latter Middle Ages. This tradition developed as the church defined its perspective on transubstantiation and as Eucharistic adoration became more common. By lifting up the elements, the priest demonstrated to the congregation the importance of what was occurring during the Service of the Sacrament and gave the congregation an opportunity to genuflect (bow in reverence) while the elements were lifted up. Martin Luther defended the usefulness of this practice, though many later Lutherans rejected it. There remains a division among Lutherans today surrounding this practice. Some argue that such a gesture contributes to a superstitious approach to the nature of the Eucharistic presence, as well as a false, medieval view of the adoration of the host. Others argue that the practice is beneficial as it helps to differentiate a Lutheran from a non-realist approach to the Sacrament. Due to the true presence of Christ, the consecration is a holy moment, and the lifting up of the elements demonstrates to the congregation the holiness of what is occurring.

Eucharistic Adoration
The practice of the elevation brings up the question of Eucharistic adoration. Though Eucharistic adoration is not documented in the early church, in the Western church throughout the Middle Ages, increasing attention was given to the uniqueness of Christ's sacramental presence and the proper response of the worshipping community. Since transubstantiation became the predominant perspective, and such a change was said to occur at the moment of consecration, many argued that Christ's body and blood should be adored. The logic is as follows: Christ is to be worshipped. The bread and wine become Christ's body and blood. Therefore, the consecrated elements should be worshipped. Though the insistence on sacramental realism is admirable, such reasoning led to a number of unhelpful practices in the Roman tradition.

Eucharistic adoration remains important in the Roman Catholic Church. It is argued that the bread and wine remain the body and blood of Christ even after the service of the Holy Eucharist. These elements, following the service, must be treated with reverence and adoration. Consecrated hosts, if not consumed, are placed into a golden box called a tabernacle. It has this name due to the conviction that God is present in the elements. Other times, hosts are displayed visibly, being placed in a standing golden object called a monstrance. When placed in the monstrance, the host is to be worshipped before the altar.

The elements are not adored simply in the context of the service of Holy Communion. They are to be adored at all times. The practice of perpetual adoration is common, wherein the host is worshipped continually. There are specific services for the sole purpose of adoration, when the reception of the elements does not occur. In various convents and monasteries, the Eucharist is adored twenty-four hours a day. This practice occurs in some parishes also, as laity volunteer to be present to adore the host at a variety of hours. Sometimes the worship of the host outside of the Mass is called Eucharistic meditation.

While there have, on occasion, been Lutherans who defend Eucharistic adoration, it has generally been rejected. There are two primary reasons for this rejection. First, Christ simply did not command that the Sacrament be used in such a manner. Jesus gave explicit instructions concerning how the church was to interact with the elements in Communion with the words "Take and eat" and "Take and drink." Had God desired the elements themselves to be worshipped and adored, he surely would have commanded it. To have services of adoration which ignore the very purpose for which the Sacrament was instituted (that is, to be received through eating and drinking) is disobedience to the commands of God. Second, the Roman perspective divorces Christ's presence in the Sacrament from the Mass itself. In the Lutheran tradition, Christ's presence does not remain in the elements for some indefinite period of time *after* the worship service has concluded. It is present *so that it might be consumed*; Christ is not trapped within a restricted locale for the purpose of continual adoration. Here again, the Roman practice of Eucharistic adoration contradicts the purpose for which God gave the Sacrament.

There are, however, valid forms of Eucharistic adoration which are in accord with Lutheran doctrine. While taking the Sacrament, congregants kneel in order to receive the elements. Kneeling is itself an act of worship and reverence. In this way, then, Christ is honored in the Sacrament. He is adored, however, *only in the context of reception*, and not after. Even this point has been debated within Lutheran theology among those who are receptionists and others who are consecrationists. The receptionists argue that Christ is present only during the act of receiving the Supper. This theory guards against the various errors which arose at the time of the Reformation. Consecrationists, on the other hand, contend that the body and blood of Christ are present on the altar through the words of institution. One's eating and drinking do not *make* the elements the body and blood of Christ, but one simply *receives* them as such. Though the receptionist position has been taken by some of the most eminent Lutheran theologians, many have rejected this position as inconsistent with Luther's own theology as well as with the words of Christ. When declaring the nature of the Sacrament, Christ simply says, "This *is* my body," not "This *will be* my body when you eat it." If the consecrationist position is correct (and I believe it is), then adoration is an acceptable practice, though only as one approaches the altar for the purpose of receiving the elements, and not afterward. That which is on the altar is, at that moment, the very body and blood of the Son of God.

Pax Domini

Following the words of institution, the pastor proclaims or chants, "The peace of the Lord be with you always." These words, called the *Pax Domini*, are spoken in the mode of proclamation, as a declaration of the gospel to the congregation. While saying the *Pax Domini*, the pastor may sometimes hold up the host and chalice and face the congregation. This gesture is done because the peace of the Lord is that which is given through the Eucharistic meal. God's peace is received in a tangible manner while one eats and drinks the elements.

The words spoken by the pastor echo the words of Jesus to the disciples when, following his resurrection, he declared, "Peace to you!" (John 20:26). Peace was ultimately the mission of Jesus, as it characterizes the purpose of his work of redemption. The peace proclaimed here is not an earthly peace from war or violence. Instead, it is the spiritual peace that Christ makes between God and man. Through God's declaration of justification, the enmity which exists between God and man due to sin is overcome. We have peace with God (Rom. 5:1). The same body and blood which bought that peace on the cross are present in the Sacrament.

The *Pax Domini* is ancient. Initially, it served as a sort of short benediction for those who left the sanctuary prior to the Communion service. As mentioned above, in the early church, there were several catechumens who would attend an average worship service who were in the process of learning about the faith but had not yet been baptized. Since the Lord's Supper is a meal for only the baptized, the catechumens and other visitors were dismissed prior to the reception of the Eucharist. This practice might seem rather odd to us today, as it is not common to dismiss worshippers from the service at any time. However, we still retain the essential purpose of this action by fencing the Lord's table. Holy Communion remains a meal for the baptized, and those who have not been baptized or do not share a common confession of faith with the congregation are not to receive the Sacrament. They can, however, remain in the service and receive a blessing from the minister, with the hope that they will be able, at some point in the future, to commune with the body of Christ at the altar.

Agnus Dei

After the pastor has blessed the congregation with the *Pax Domini*, the people of God sing the *Agnus Dei*. This hymn contains the words "the

Lamb of God who takes away the sins of the world." This phrase arises from the mouth of John the Baptist, who characterized the mission of the Messiah in such a manner (John 1:29). By identifying Jesus as the Lamb of God, John declared him to be the fulfillment of the Old Testament sacrifices as the all-sufficient offering for sin. Complete atonement was accomplished by Christ on the cross.

The congregation sings or speaks these words in the Communion service to recognize that it is the Lamb of God who makes himself present in the bread and wine of the Eucharistic meal. Christ's act of redemption, which consists in his taking away the sins of the world, is brought to the worshippers in their reception of the elements. Through the Sacrament, Christ gives the benefits won through his atoning death.

In this part of the service, the congregation enters into the mode of praise. Christ is thanked and adored for his redemptive work on the cross. The pastor faces the altar while singing in the priestly position. The *Agnus Dei* also serves as an act of remembrance. As Christ commanded the disciples to remember him and his redemptive work while partaking of Holy Communion, the congregation audibly remembers and confesses this work through this song. A hymn of thanksgiving and remembrance, the *Agnus Dei* ends with a request for grace. The posture of approaching God as a beggar in need of grace remains through the reception.

The singing of the *Agnus Dei* during the Communion service dates back at least to the eighth century. One reason the *Agnus Dei* occurs at this time is that it is an occasion for the pastor to receive Holy Communion before distributing the elements to his congregation. Often, various helpers in the service will also receive the Sacrament during the singing of the *Agnus Dei*. There are different practices surrounding the communing of the minister. In some congregations, the pastor self-communes as an act of cleansing prior to his giving of the Sacrament to others. Some argue, in contrast to this, that Holy Communion should always come from outside of the person receiving, and thus have someone else commune the pastor. Whatever practice is preferred, the minister should himself receive Communion before distributing it to others.

CHAPTER 13:
The RECEPTION of HOLY COMMUNION

The most important aspect of the Service of the Sacrament is the reception of the elements by the people of God. The consecration never stands alone, and it is never to be done without the intention of the actual eating and drinking of Christ's body and blood. There are several differences among congregations concerning exactly how the elements are to be distributed. In many congregations, there is an altar rail, and as members come forward they kneel in order to receive the Sacrament. This is the preferred manner of reception because the people come to God in a position of humility and adoration by taking this posture. In other congregations, particularly large ones, lines are formed in which the elements are received while standing.

Receiving Both Elements
One of the most important pastoral concerns during the era of the Reformation was that the people of God receive both Christ's body and blood in the worship service. In the Western medieval church, it became common for believers to receive only the host while celebrating Holy Communion. As superstition arose surrounding the Lord's Supper, there began to be fear around the partaking of wine in the service. If laity were allowed to take the cup, it was easy for Christ's blood to be spilled on the ground. Due to those fears, and some other theological convictions about the necessity of receiving only the host, the wine became the special privilege of the priest. This practice changed in Roman Catholicism only in recent times.

There were two concerns driving these convictions in the Roman Church which the Lutheran reformers were sensitive to. First, theologians argued that Christ's body and blood were both present in in the host as well as in the wine. After all, a body does contain blood, and Christ's body, soul, and divinity are in the host. This point is to be granted, but it does not negate Christ's institution of drinking of the cup as part of the Lord's Supper. Second, both traditions were concerned that the blood of Christ not be treated just as common wine. The Lutherans were not willing to say, however, that this concern should negate the drinking of Christ's blood by the laity.

The argument put forward by the Reformers for the necessity of receiving the Sacrament under both kinds was rather simple. Christ commanded that his disciples do two things: take and eat, and take and drink. No amount of theological argumentation or rational polemics can make void the clear words of Christ. Had Christ not desired the church to partake of both elements, he would not have commanded the opposite. The church does not, at any point, have the authority to disobey the clear commands of Christ. In this instance, the Roman Church had done so. If Jesus said to do it, we must do it.

Individual Cups Versus the Common Cup
For the majority of the church's history, the people partook of the Sacrament from one single cup. The chalice served as the only instrument of receiving the blood of Christ. However, in recent years, largely due to fears about germs, many churches have begun using individual cups to administer the Sacrament. This change has led to a variety of practices in congregations. In some, either the common cup or the individual cups are used exclusively, and in others, the option is given for each communicant to decide which method to use.

There are significant theological reasons why the common cup is the preferred method of partaking of Holy Communion. The first is that there is theological significance to the single cup that all people drink from. When writing to the Corinthians, Paul mentions that there is one cup that the congregants partake of (1 Cor. 10:16). This single cup emphasizes the fact that the Sacrament is not an individualistic practice. When partaking of the body and blood of Christ, one is not doing so in isolation, but with Christ's entire body. Just as the Sacrament is a sharing in Christ, it is also a sharing in the community of the church.

The second major concern with the practice of using individual cups is the manner in which those cups are cleaned or disposed of. When the Sacrament is celebrated, God uses ordinary wine for a special purpose. It is the instrument through which God's people receive Christ's blood. With that being the case, the wine itself should be treated with great reverence even after the service is ended. This does not mean that one needs to treat it superstitiously or believe that the elements remain Christ's body and blood for some indefinite period of time following the service. Nonetheless, because of its place in worship, the wine remains a sacred thing, and it should be disposed of in a reverent manner. When a common cup alone is used, it is a common practice for all of the wine to be consumed by the pastor or assisting deacons during the service so that the elements are not mistreated after the service. When individual cups are utilized, the wine can still be consumed, or it can be poured onto the ground, just as Christ's blood was poured onto the ground in his crucifixion. The problem, however, is that it is nearly impossible to clean out all of the wine from the small cups.

Another problem is with the manner in which the cups themselves are treated after the service. A chalice is a sturdy instrument which is cleaned after each service and placed away somewhere to be used again. In other words, it remains set apart for this holy purpose. The individual cups, however, are often plastic and cheap, and they are simply thrown into the trash after the service. Is this really the best way to honor Christ's blood—by using cups that we just throw into the trash? If individual cups are used, it is better to use glass cups which can be cleaned and then reused in the future.

Intinction
A debate exists surrounding the proper manner in which to receive the wine in the Sacrament. For the majority of communicants in Lutheran congregations, the wine is drunk apart from the host. However, another practice exists which is called *intinction*. This involves dipping the host into the wine, so that the wine is not received by drinking, but instead by means of the bread. Though this may seem like a harmless practice, there are reasons to refrain from doing it.

There are two kinds of intinction. In the Roman tradition, the priest intincts, and the communicant's hand never actually touches the host. Instead, it is placed directly onto the tongue. In some Anglican and other Protestant churches, the communicant dips the host into the wine and then eats. The problem with this practice, in either form, is that is simply does not act in obedience with Christ's own words. At the institution of the Lord's Supper, Jesus did not say to the disciples, "Take and dip my body into my blood," but instead he commanded, "Take and drink!" There simply is no reason to ignore Christ's own prescribed manner of receiving the Supper and implement something else.

It is all too common that churches try to innovate where the Sacrament is concerned. Many Baptist churches, for example, use grape juice instead of wine in Holy Communion. Jesus, however, most certainly did not have access to Welch's grape juice, but he gave his disciples actual wine. This much is especially clear in that what the Corinthians were drinking was able to get them drunk (1 Cor. 11:21)! While there certainly are exceptions for things like gluten intolerance and alcohol allergies, when possible, the Supper should follow the pattern that Jesus himself established.

CHAPTER 14:
POST-COMMUNION SERVICE

The post-Communion service is the final aspect of worship. The congregation has just received Christ's body and blood as the climax of the service. God has come down to earth on the altar, through which divine action God's people have received forgiveness and life. Just as in the rest of the service, the dialogue between God and man continues here. After God has bestowed his gifts in the Sacrament, the congregation responds again with praise and thanksgiving.

The Blessing
It is customary for the pastor to pronounce a blessing upon each group of communicants who approach the altar following their reception of the Sacrament. Though there is no one standard blessing, it takes the form of something like this: "May this true body and blood strengthen you and keep you steadfast in the true faith unto life everlasting." This blessing is accompanied by the sign of the cross, because in this meal, the church has communed with the Triune God through the fruits of Christ's death. The blessing serves as a reminder of the power of this sacrament, that it is not a mere symbol but a powerful act of the Triune God.

A blessing is often pronounced also on those who approach the altar who are not receiving the Supper—often young children who have not yet been instructed or Christians who have not yet confessed the faith of the congregation. These people should come up to the rail along with the rest of the church so that the pastor might bless them in accordance with their baptism.

Post-Communion Prayer
Every act of grace should be responded to with prayer and thanksgiving. A prayer of thanks following the reception of the Sacrament has been customary from the earliest days of the church. The *Didache*, the earliest Christian document we have available that describes the worship service (though not in great detail), mentions that a prayer of thanksgiving always followed the Supper. The post-Communion prayer follows the

Jewish custom of thanksgiving prayers during the Passover celebration.

There are generally two parts to a post-Communion prayer. First, the pastor thanks God for the blessings that were given in the Sacrament, such as the forgiveness of sins and spiritual nourishment. Second, the pastor often implores God to use this Sacrament to the benefit of those receiving it. The Sacrament empowers Christians to live as God's sanctified people throughout the week as it guards them against the attacks of the devil and helps them to grow in Christian love. These two aspects of the prayer are general guidelines because a number of post-Communion prayers are used by different traditions.

Post-Communion Hymn

Following the prayer is an opportunity for the people of God to continue giving thanks to God through song. This action follows the pattern established in the Old Testament, wherein psalms were composed and sung at appropriate times of thanksgiving. There are a variety of options for hymns to be used in this portion of the service. A song commonly used in Lutheran churches in recent years is titled (appropriately) "Thank the Lord." This hymn is an expression of praise for the gifts of Christ and an admonition to tell the world of the wonderful blessings of God's grace.

A second hymn that is often used in Lutheran Communion services is the *Nunc Dimittis* from Luke 2:29–32. While this song is universally used among liturgical churches, only the Lutheran tradition places it here. In other churches, it is most often used in either Compline or Vespers services rather than on Sunday mornings. The *Nunc Dimittis* comes from the faithful Jewish believer Simeon following his encountering Jesus at the Temple. God had promised Simeon that he would see the Messiah with his own eyes prior to death, and after this experience, Simeon asks that he would be able to depart from this life in peace. As the congregation sings this song, the people acknowledge that, like Simeon, they have encountered Christ. With their own eyes, they have seen the salvation that God has prepared through this holy Sacrament. Congregants ask to depart from the service in peace in light of this salvation.

Benediction

Every service ends with a benediction, even if Holy Communion is not celebrated. The benediction serves as a final blessing given to the people of God before they depart from the church. This is the final formal aspect of worship and signals the end of the service. The benediction is a word of proclamation, meaning that it is directed toward the congregation. For this reason, the pastor faces not the altar but the people. The benediction is not a request or prayer to God that the people might be blessed, but it is rather a declaration that God's blessing *is* upon his people who are gathered together. As such, the benediction is a word of gospel. Just as the service begins with the gospel through the words of invocation, it ends in the same manner. In the Christian life, everything begins and ends with God's action, not ours.

The practice of using a benediction in worship comes directly from Scripture. The Aaronic benediction recorded in Numbers 6:22–26 was a regular part of Jewish worship, and the same blessing is often proclaimed in churches today. The New Testament similarly includes benedictions (Heb. 13:20–21, 2 Thess. 2:16–17, Eph. 6:23–24). The church often uses these same New Testament words to end worship today. After the birth of Christianity, benedictions began to receive a strongly Trinitarian form, as is evident in 2 Corinthians 13:14. The benediction, then, strongly mirrors the invocation which begins the service. The service begins and ends with the proclamation of the Triune God's presence and blessings. While pronouncing the benediction, the pastor motions in the sign of the cross, and congregants are encouraged to do the same.

A benediction may be either spoken or chanted. The congregation usually responds to the benediction by speaking in unison or singing, "Amen." By saying this, the church is affirming that what the pastor has spoken is true: God's blessing is with his people.

Recessional and Closing Hymn
If the service has a processional at the beginning, it will similarly end with a recessional. Just as the processional signals the entrance of God's presence into the sanctuary, so the recessional demonstrates his going out into the world. The candles on the altar (or beside the altar) are snuffed out, and the acolyte carries the flame out of the sanctuary. This action signifies not simply God's departure from the church but also his entrance into the world outside of the church. Just as the light of Christ entered into the sanctuary with the people of God, so does his light leave the sanctuary, so that worshippers might bring that light to the world around them. The order in which individuals enter the sanctuary for the procession remains the same for the recession. The cross leads the way, and as it is carried down the aisle, congregants turn to face the cross as

it exits the sanctuary. This gesture signals, again, that the cross is at the very center of the worship life of the church, as the last thing that people contemplate before exiting the sanctuary is Christ's crucifixion.

A hymn is sung at the close of the service. Just as God's people enter into his house with songs of thanksgiving and praise, so do they leave in the same manner. This is the final act of thanksgiving sung in response to the proclamation of God's blessing in the benediction, as well as to the entirety of the service. The final hymn, generally, should be joyful in tone as the people leave rejoicing in the good news of the gospel. The tone may me more restrained, however, during the penitential seasons of Lent and Advent. Like the other two hymns, this one should reflect the themes of the church year and of the service that particular Sunday.

CONCLUSION

There is no Christianity without worship. Worship is the very heartbeat of the church, and unfortunately, we do not often give the subject the attention that it deserves. This treatment has been only cursory, giving some explanation of the basic elements of the Divine Service. If you desire to delve deeper into the subject, I would encourage you to read some of the books included in the bibliography. Without an understanding of why we worship in the manner we do other than a simple appeal to tradition, we are likely to lose these traditions. However, when the church once again discovers the riches of historic, biblical, liturgical worship, the church will be reinvigorated in its mission. Strong worship also leads to strong theology.

Not every congregation will include every aspect of worship as outlined in this book. Liturgy often differs from congregation to congregation. One should not expect any church to do things perfectly in the exact way we would like it to. For pastors, it is extremely hard to implement or change elements in worship where a different practice has been used for decades. Changes take time, and often many years. These changes can happen only, however, when we are willing to teach and willing to learn. Liturgy should not be in a constant state of flux due to the personal preference of the current pastor at any given congregation.

It is my hope that this work will do some small part in helping the church to understand the riches of liturgical worship. Do not just keep these truths to yourself, but teach them to others. It is only through the process of catechesis that such riches can be retained.

Bibliography

Andreopoulos, Andreas. *The Sign of the Cross: The Gesture, the Mystery, the History*. Brewster, MA: Paraclete, 2006.

Atkerson, Stephen E. *House Church-Simple-Strategic-Scriptural*. Atlanta: New Testament Reformation, 2008.

Aulen, Gustaf. *Eucharist and Sacrifice*. Translated by Eric H. Wahlstrom. Philadelphia: Muhlenberg, 1956.

Baker, Kenneth. *Fundamentals of Catholicism*. San Francisco: Ignatius, 1982.

Barth, Karl. *Protestant Theology in the Nineteenth Century*. Translated by Brian Cozens and John Bowden. London: SCM, 1972.

Bergendoff, Conrad. *The Church of the Lutheran Reformation: A Historical Survey of Lutheranism*. St. Louis: Concordia Publishing House, 1967.

Biermann, Joel. *A Case for Character: Towards a Lutheran Virtue Ethics*. Minneapolis: Fortress, 2014.

Brauer, Leonard James and Fred L. Precht. *Lutheran Worship: History and Practice*. St. Louis: Concordia Publishing House, 1993.

Brighton, Louis A. *Revelation*. Concordia Commentary. St. Louis: Concordia, 1999.

Brown, Peter. *The Cult of the Saints: Its Rise and Function in Latin Christianity*. Chicago: University of Chicago Press, 1982.

Brunner, Peter. *Worship in the Name of Jesus*. Translated by M. H. Bertram. St. Louis: Concordia Publishing House, 1968.

Bushell, Michael. *Songs of Zion: A Contemporary Case for Exclusive Psalmody*. Pittsburgh: Crown & Covenant, 2011.

Calvin, John. *Institutes of the Christian Religion*. Edited by John T. McNeill. Louisville: Westminster Press, 1960.

Chemnitz, Martin and Jacob Andreae. *Church Order for Braunschweig-Wolfenbuttel: How Doctrine, Ceremonies, and Other Church-Related Matters Shall (By God's Grace) Be Conducted Henceforth*. In *Chemnitz's Works*, vol. 9. Translated by Jacob Corzine, Matthew C. Harrison, and Andrew Smith. St. Louis: Concordia Publishing House, 2015.

Chemnitz, Martin. *Examination of the Council of Trent*. Vol 1. Translated by Fred Kramer. St. Louis: Concordia, 1971.

Chytraeus, David. *On Sacrifice: A Reformation Treatise in Biblical Theology*. Translated by John Warwick Montgomery. St. Louis: Concordia Publishing House, 1962.

The Commission on Worship of The Lutheran Church—Missouri Synod. *Lutheran Service Book*. St. Louis: Concordia Publishing House, 2006.

Cooper, Jordan. *Baptized into Christ: A Guide to the Christian Life*. Watseka, IL: Just and Sinner, 2016.

———. "A Lutheran Response to *Justification: Five Views*." *LOGIA Online* (blog). LOGIA, July 31, 2012. https://logia.org/logia-online/216.

———. *Christification: A Lutheran Approach to Theosis*. Eugene, OR: Wipf and Stock, 2014.

———. *The Great Divide: A Lutheran Evaluation of Reformed Theology*. Eugene, OR: Wipf and Stock, 2015.

———. *The Righteousness of One: An Evaluation of Early Patristic Soteriology in Light of the New Perspective on Paul*. Eugene, OR: Wipf and Stock, 2013.

Courvoisier, Jaques. *Zwingli: A Reformed Theologian*. Richmond: John

Knox, 1961.

DeVries, Dave. "Becoming a Self Feeder." *Missional Challenge.* https://www.missionalchallenge.com/becoming-a-self-feeder/

Dunlop, Colin. *Anglican Public Worship.* Eugene, OR: Wipf and Stock, 2012.

Eire, Carlos M. N. *War Against the Idols: The Reformation of Worship from Erasmus to Calvin.* New York: Cambridge University Press, 1989.

"Eucharistic Prayer I (Roman Canon)." *Mass of the 1970 Missal.* As found in The Catholic Liturgical Library. http://www.catholicliturgy.com/index.cfm/fuseaction/text/index/4/subindex/67/contentindex/22/start/9.

Fee, Gordon D. *Pauline Christology: An Exegetical-Theological Study.* Grand Rapids: Baker, 2013.

Finney, Charles G. *Autobiography: The Story of America's Greatest Evangelist—In His Own Words.* Bloomington, MN: Bethany House, 2006.

Forde, Gerhard. *Theology Is for Proclamation.* Minneapolis: Fortress, 1990.

Foster, Douglad A. *The Encyclopedia of the Stone-Campbell Movement.* Grad Rapids: Eerdmans, 2012.

Frame, John. *A Fresh Look at the Regulative Principle: A Broader View.* Frame-Poythress.org. June 4, 2012. http://www.frame-poythress.org/a-fresh-look-at-the-regulative-principle-a-broader-view/.

Franzmann, Martin H. *The Revelation to John.* St. Louis: Concordia, 1975.

Ghezzi, Bert. *The Sign of the Cross: Recovering the Power of the Ancient Prayer.* Chicago: Loyola, 2004.

Gore, R. J. *Covenantal Worship: Reconsidering the Puritan Regulative Principle.* Phillipsburg: P & R, 2002.

Grabbe, Lester L. *An Introduction to First Century Judaism: Jewish Religion and History in the Second Temple Period.* New York: Bloomsbury, 1996.

Harless, Adolf von. *A System of Christian Ethics.* Watseka, IL: Just and Sinner, 2014.

Hahn, Scott. *The Lamb's Supper: The Mass as Heaven on Earth.* Doubleday, 1999.

Hippolytus. *On the Apostolic Tradition.* Popular Patristic Series. Translated by Alistair Stewart-Sykes. Yonkers, NY: St. Vladimir's, 2015.

Holmes, Michael W., ed. and trans. *The Apostolic Fathers: Greek Texts and English Translations.* Grand Rapids: Baker, 1992.

Hopko, Thomas. *Worship.* The Orthodox Faith Volume 2. Syosset, NY: OCA, 1997.

Horton, Michael S. "Creeds and Deeds: How Doctrine Leads to Doxological Living." *Modern Reformation* 15, no. 6 (November 2006). https://www.whitehorseinn.org/article/creeds-and-deeds/.

Hurtado, Larry W. *At the Origins of Christian Worship: The Context and Character of Earliest Christian Devotion.* Grand Rapids: Eerdmans, 1999.

Hyun, Yung Hoon. *Redemptive-Historical Hermeneutics and Homiletics: Debates in Holland, America, and Korea from 1930 to 2012.* Eugene, OR: Wipf and Stock, 2015.

Irenaeus of Lyon. *Against Heresies Book 3.* Translated by Matthew C. Steenberg. Mahwah, NJ: Paulist, 2012.

John of Damascus. *On the Divine Images: Three Apologies Against those who Attack the Divine Images.* Translated by David Anderson. Crestwood, NY: St. Vladimir's Seminary Press, 1980.

Jungmann, Josef A. *The Early Liturgy: To the Time of Gregory the Great.* Translated by Francis A. Brunner. London: Darton, Longman & Todd, 1959.

Just, Arthur A. *Heaven on Earth: The Gifts of Christ in the Divine Service.* St. Louis: Concordia Publishing House, 2008.

———. *The Ongoing Feast: Table Fellowship and Eschatology at Emmaus.* Collegeville, MN: Liturgical Press, 1993.

The Ante-Nicene Fathers. Edited by Alexander Roberts and James Donaldson. 10 vols. Peabody, MA: Hendrickson, 1994.

Kant, Immanuel. *Religion within the Limits of Reason Alone.* San Francisco: HarperOne, 2008.

Kleinig, John A. *Leviticus.* Concordia Commentary Series. St. Louis: Concordia, 2003.

Kolb, Robert and Timothy J. Wengert. *The Book of Concord: The Confessions of the Evangelical Lutheran Church.* Minneapolis: Fortress Press, 2000.

Krauth, Charles Porterfield. *The Conservative Reformation and Its Theology.* St. Louis: Concordia Publishing House, 2007.

Kretzmann, Paul E. *Christian Art: Its Place and Use in Lutheran Worship.* St. Louis: Concordia Publishing House, 1921.

Leithart, Peter J. *The Baptized Body.* Moscow, ID: Canon, 2007.

———. *Blessed Are the Hungry: Meditations on the Lord's Supper.* Moscow, ID: Canon, 2000.

Lightsey, Pamela R. *Our Lives Matter: A Womanist Queer Theology.* Eugene, OR: Pickwick, 2015.

Lotz, David W. *Ritschl and Luther: A Fresh Perspective on Albrecht Ritschl's Theology in the Light of His Luther Study.* Nashville: Abingdon, 1974.

Luther, Martin. *Luther's Small Catechism with Explanation.* St. Louis: Concordia Publishing House, 1991.

Marquart, Kurt. "Confessions and Ceremonies." In *A Contemporary Look at the Formula of Concord*, edited by Robert D. Preus and Wilbert H. Rosin, 260–70. St. Louis: Concordia Publishing House, 1978.

Mathison, Keith A. *Given for You: Reclaiming Calvin's Doctrine of the Lord's Supper*. Phillipsburg, NJ: P&R, 2002.

Meyers, Jeffrey J. *The Lord's Service: The Grace of Covenant Renewal Worship*. Moscow, ID: Canon, 2003.

Moltmann, Jurgen. *Theology of Hope*. Minneapolis: Fortress, 1993.

Morales, Michael L. *Who Shall Ascend the Mountain of the Lord?: A Biblical Theology of the Book of Leviticus*. Downers Grove, IL: IVP, 2015.

Moseley, Allan. *Exalting Jesus in Leviticus*. Christ-Centered Exposition Commentary. Nashville: Holman Reference, 2015.

Pipa, Joseph A. *The Lord's Day*. Fearn, Ross-Shire: Christian Focus, 1996.

Poellot, Luther. *Revelation*. Concordia Classic Commentary Series. St. Louis: Concordia Publishing House, 1962.

Reed, Luther D. *The Lutheran Liturgy: A Study of the Common Liturgy of the Lutheran Church in America*. Philadelphia: Fortress, 1947.

Remensnyder, Junius Benjamin. *The Lutheran Manual*. New York: Boschen and Wefer, 1983.

Rhegius, Urbanus. *Preaching the Reformation: The Homiletical Handbook of Urbanus Rhegius*. Edited and translated by Scott H. Hendrix. Milwaukee: Marquette University Press, 2003.

Ritche, Daniel F.N. *The Regulative Principle of Worship: Explained and Applied*. Maitland, FL: Xulon, 2007.

Roth, John D. *Practices: Mennonite Worship and Witness*. Harrisonburg, VA: Herald, 2009.

Rudolph, Kurt. *Gnosis: the Nature and History of Gnosticism.* San Francisco: HarperOne, 1987.

Sasse, Hermann. *This is My Body: Luther's Contention for the Real Presence in the Sacrament of the Altar.* Eugene, OR: Wipf and Stock, 2001.

Scaer, David P. *Law and Gospel and the Means of Grace.* St. Louis: Luther Academy, 2008.

Schweitzer, Albert. *The Quest of the Historical Jesus: A Critical Study of Its Progress from Reimarus to Wrede.* New York: Macmillan, 1968.

Schwertley, Brian M. *Exclusive Psalmody: A Biblical Defense.* Kearney, NE: Morris, 2002.

Seiss, Joseph A. *Holy Types: Or The Gospel in Leviticus; A Series of Lectures on the Hebrew Ritual.* Philadelphia: General Council, 1917.

Senn, Frank. *Christian Liturgy: Catholic and Evangelical.* Minneapolis: Fortress, 1997.

———. *Introduction to Christian Liturgy.* Minneapolis, Fortress: 2012.

Siecienski, A. Edward. *The Filioque: The History of a Doctrinal Controversy.* London: Oxford, 2012.

Sklar, Jay. *Leviticus.* Tyndale Old Testament Commentaries. Downers Grove, IL: IVPS, 2014.

Stuckwisch, D. Richard. *Philip Melanchthon and the Lutheran Confession of Eucharistic Sacrifice.* Bynum, TX: Repristination, 1997.

Stuhlman, Byron D. *Eucharistic Celebration 1789–1979.* New York: Church Hymnal Corporation, 1988.

Sundburg, Walter. *Worship as Repentance: Lutheran Liturgical Tradition and Catholic Consensus.* Grand Rapids: Eerdmans, 2012.

USA National Committee of the Lutheran World Federation and the Bishops' Committee for Ecumenical and Interreligious Affairs. *Lutherans and Catholic in Dialogue III: The Eucharist as Sacrifice.* Washington, DC, 1967.

Webber, Christopher L. *A User's Guide to the Holy Eucharist Rites I & II.* Harrisburg, PA: Morehouse, 1997.

Wengert, Timothy. *Priesthood, Pastors, Bishops: Public Ministry for the Reformation and Today.* Minneapolis: Fortress, 2008.

Whitaker, E. C. *Documents of the Baptismal Liturgy.* London: SPCK Publishing, 1960.

Wieting, Kenneth W. *The Blessings of Weekly Communion.* St. Louis: Concordia Publishing House, 2006.

Zeedon, Walter Ernst and Kevin G. Walker. *Faith and Act: The Survival of Medieval Ceremonies in the Lutheran Reformation.* St. Louis: Concordia Publishing House, 2012.

Glossary of Terms

Absolution. The declaration of the minister that the sins of the penitent are forgiven.

Advent. The season prior to the celebration of Christmas, wherein believers prepare themselves, through repentance, for the celebration of Christ's incarnation.

Agnus Dei. A song used prior to the reception of Holy Communion in which Christ is spoken of as the Lamb of God who takes away the sins of the world.

Alb. A white robe worn by the minister during worship. It is also used by acolytes, lectors, and Communion helpers.

All Saints Day. The Sunday following Reformation, whereon the saints of all times are honored.

Alleluia. A word that means "praise Yahweh." This word is included in several hymns and is sung prior to the gospel reading. It is omitted during penitential seasons.

Anamnesis. A prayer of remembrance, wherein the acts of Christ are recited.

Ascension, Feast of. The celebration of Christ's assumption into heaven following his resurrection.

Benediction. The closing blessing given by the minister to the congregation. It ends the worship service and leads to the closing hymn.

Cassock. A long, black, form-fitting robe worn by pastors and seminarians. This used to be the standard wear of all pastors and priests.

Chasuble. A poncho-like robe worn over an alb for the celebration of

Holy Communion.

Christ the King Sunday. The final Sunday of the church year, when Christ is honored as king.

Christmas. A twelve-day celebration of Christ's incarnation and birth.

Cincture. A rope or band that the pastor ties around his alb.

Clerical shirt. The daily clothing of many ministers. This shirt, which has either a white tab in front, or a white band which goes around the neck, marks a pastor as such. It is a uniform, like uniforms worn by people in other professions to mark their unique vocations.

Collect. See "Prayer of the day."

Confession. The act of declaring one's sins against God. This happens at the beginning of the worship service or in a private meeting with the pastor.

Consecrationism. The view that the body and blood of Christ are present in the bread and wine at the time of consecration.

Daily office. The practice of singing or praying psalms at specific times in the day.

Easter. The day the church celebrates Christ's resurrection. Also, a fifty-day season beginning with Easter Day and continuing until Pentecost.

Elevation of the host. The practice of raising up the host following the words of institution.

Entrance hymn. The first hymn in the worship service, accompanying the processional.

Epiclesis. The invocation of the Holy Spirit during the celebration of Holy Communion.

Eucharist. A name for Holy Communion that means "thanksgiving."

Eucharistic adoration. The Roman Catholic practice of honoring and adoring the host, even outside of the reception of Holy Communion.

Eucharistic prayers. The various prayers that accompany the celebration of Holy Communion, including the thanksgiving, anamnesis, and epiclesis.

Gloria in Excelsis. A hymn taken from Luke 2:14 which follows the *Kyrie*.

Gospel book. A large volume containing the four gospels, used during a gospel procession.

Gospel procession. For the gospel reading, the minister enters into the congregation as an assistant carries and holds a gospel book.

Hymn of the day. The second hymn in the service, which is sung prior to the sermon.

Intinction. The practice of dipping the host into the wine when receiving the Lord's Supper.

Introit. A section of a psalm used near the beginning of the service, connected to the lectionary readings of that day.

Invocation. The announcement that God is present in the worship service: "In the name of the Father, the Son, and the Holy Spirit."

Kyrie. A prayer that is chanted and includes the phrase "Lord have mercy."

Lectionary. A series of appointed readings for each Sunday of the church year; the readings for each day are selected from multiple books of the Bible.

Lent. The forty-day season prior to Easter. This is a time of repentance, fasting, and spiritual discipline.

Monstrance. A golden stand, used in Roman Catholicism, which holds the host for the purpose of Eucharistic adoration.

Orans position. The raised position in which the pastor holds his hands while praying on behalf of the congregation.

Pax Domini. The proclamation, "The peace of the Lord be with you always," which follows the words of institution.

Pentecost. The feast observed fifty days after Easter when the church celebrates the gift of the Holy Spirit.

Post-Communion Prayer. A prayer of thanksgiving which follows the reception of the Lord's Supper.

Prayer of the day. A prayer following the *Gloria* that changes depending on the time and theme of the church year. It is also referred to as the "collect."

Preface. The first part of the Service of the Sacrament, from the preface dialogue through the singing of the *Sanctus*.

Preface dialogue. The first part of the preface, wherein the minister and congregation speak to one another.

Procession. The act whereby the pastor and helpers in the worship service walk into the sanctuary and up to the altar during the opening hymn.

Processional cross. A cross on a pole which is carried in the service at the front of the procession. It then leads the recession out of the service.

Proper preface. The lengthy prayer spoken by the minister following the preface dialogue. It changes throughout the church year to suit various liturgical seasons.

Receptionism. The view that Christ's body and blood are present only when one receives the bread and wine.

Recession. The act wherein the pastor and assistants depart from the chancel into the back of the church.

Regulative principle of worship. The Reformed perspective on worship, which states that only things which have been directly commanded should be done in the worship service.

Saints' days. Various days set aside during the year to remember important figures in Scripture and the history of the church.

Salutation. The opening greeting of the minister, wherein he says, "The Lord be with you" to the congregation. The congregation responds, "And also with you."

Sanctus. The singing of "Holy, holy, holy" that follows the proper preface.

Service of the Sacrament. The second part of the worship service, which surrounds the celebration of Holy Communion.

Service of the Word. The first section in the worship service, which centers on the proclamation of God's Word.

Stole. A scarf-shaped vestment which is worn by the minister. The color worn changes depending on the time of the church year. The stole is a symbol of ordination.

Tabernacle. A box on the altar utilized to hold the bread used in Holy Communion in Roman Catholic churches.

"This Is the Feast." A modern hymn used as a hymn of praise in place of the *Gloria*.

Transfiguration, Feast of. The commemoration of the event in Christ's life whereupon his identity is revealed to the disciples alongside the appearance of Moses and Elijah.

Transubstantiation. The Roman Catholic teaching that the bread and wine used in Communion become Christ's body and blood, while the physical elements of bread and wine cease to exist.

Trinity Sunday. The Sunday following Pentecost, when God is honored as Father, Son, and Holy Spirit.

Verba. The words of institution used in Holy Communion.

Verba nuda. This term refers to the practice of using only the words of institution during the Eucharistic service, without Eucharistic prayers.

Words of institution. The words of Christ which are spoken over the elements, through which God sanctifies the elements.

Made in the USA
Coppell, TX
19 March 2022